TOWNSHIP OF UNION
FREE PU

D0679526

I FEEL GOOD

JAMES BROWN

I FEEL GOOD

A Memoir of a Life of Soul

WITH AN INTRODUCTION BY

Marc Eliot

NAL NEW AMERICAN LIBRARY

TOWNSHIP OF UNION
FREE PUBLIC LIBRARY

New American Library
Published by New American Library, a division of
Penguin Group (USA) Inc., 375 Hudson Street,
New York, New York 10014, USA
Penguin Group (Canada), 10 Alcorn Avenue, Toronto,
Ontario M4V 3B2, Canada (a division of Pearson Penguin Canada Inc.)
Penguin Books Ltd., 80 Strand, London WC2R 0RL, England
Penguin Ireland, 25 St. Stephen's Green, Dublin 2,
Ireland (a division of Penguin Books Ltd.)
Penguin Group (Australia), 250 Camberwell Road, Camberwell, Victoria 3124,
Australia (a division of Pearson Australia Group Pty. Ltd.)
Penguin Books India Pvt. Ltd., 11 Community Centre, Panchsheel Park,
New Delhi – 110 017, India
Penguin Group (NZ), cnr Airborne and Rosedale Roads, Albany,
Auckland 1310, New Zealand (a division of Pearson New Zealand Ltd.)
Penguin Books (South Africa) (Pty.) Ltd., 24 Sturdee Avenue,
Rosebank, Johannesburg 2196, South Africa

Penguin Books Ltd., Registered Offices:
80 Strand, London WC2R 0RL, England

First published by New American Library,
a division of Penguin Group (USA) Inc.

First Printing, January 2005
10 9 8 7 6 5 4 3 2 1

Copyright © James Brown, 2005
All rights reserved

NEW AMERICAN LIBRARY and logo are trademarks of Penguin Group (USA) Inc.

LIBRARY OF CONGRESS CATALOGING-IN-PUBLICATION DATA

Brown, James
    I feel good / by James Brown ; with an introduction by Marc Eliot.
      p.   cm.
    ISBN 0-451-21393-9 (nal hardcover : alk. paper)
    1. Brown, James.   2. Soul musicians—United States—Biography.   I. Eliot, Marc.
II. Title.
    ML420.B818A3   2002
    782.421644'092—dc22   2004024368

Printed in the United States of America

Without limiting the rights under copyright reserved above, no part of this publication may
be reproduced, stored in or introduced into a retrieval system, or transmitted, in any form, or
by any means (electronic, mechanical, photocopying, recording, or otherwise), without the
prior written permission of both the copyright owner and the above publisher of this book.

The scanning, uploading, and distribution of this book via the Internet or via any other
means without the permission of the publisher is illegal and punishable by law. Please purchase only authorized electronic editions, and do not participate in or encourage electronic
piracy of copyrighted materials. Your support of the author's rights is appreciated.

INTRODUCTION

by MARC ELIOT

FOR MANY OF THOSE SO-CALLED BABY BOOMERS WHO grew up poor, fast, and tough on the mean streets of America's grittiest cities, James Brown was their first living cultural icon. By the time they were barely old enough to tune in a radio, they had discovered the most soulful music available anywhere, filled with a rhythmic bravado that taught them about the unwritten laws of self-respect, the reverential treatment of women, the pursuit of their own happiness, and perhaps most important, the savvy to survive while doing so.

The collective imagination of his appearance was surpassed only by the reality of it. From the first time he took to the stage, James Brown struck just the right balance of bravado and bathos in his fancy dress clothes; no matter

1

what the occasion, he always came on sugar-free, strong but never sweet.

He danced like a fighter even as he moved through his songs like a dancer. *And what moves!* He could shake his way around the edge of a dime and never lose the smile on his face. His stature was defined by the music he made, which shaped the cultural bylaws a generation lived by and for, sending a message that cut across race, color, creed, and style. He has often said that from the beginning he intended never to compromise his talent—to express himself in the raw, untamed way that came to define James Brown, at a level of intensity and truth that most performers would not, or could not, attain or would never risk trying to.

The difference was obvious. Most of the other performers around worked for commercial acceptance; he wanted an emotional connection. The scream, the moan, the moves—he put them all out there and that *was* the message, even if it made some in the audience (and others in the industry, and still others in government) uncomfortable with it and him. With his handsome face and his high fancy Dixie-peach'd pomp, he had a look that harnessed an irresistible force that propelled him to greatness. And he could express in the most meaningful fashion what we were feeling as we wafted through our jean-aged years heading straight for the coming cyclone of adulthood. It was a testament to his true artistry that James Brown's music delivered a message that cut right to the nexus of our souls—a message of hope and reconciliation, as well as love and sex, that put him above all others, that made him *numero uno,* the primo street-corner cat. His scream was the collective measure of our scream, the one that still lurks inside all of us but that we don't always know how to release. The origin of his music was the origin of everyone's music, his pain everyone's pain, and his sense of pride the badge of a generation.

The pop culture legacy of James Brown continues to flow like the muddy waters of a great river of soul, rock, pop, and funk, into the many streams it has become today in the sounds of rap, house, and hip-hop. As everything must come from something, that river's origins may be traced to the spirited sounds of Louis Jordan; to the sweet tinkling of Nat "King" Cole; to the celebrated splits of thirteen-year-old Frankie Lymon at Allan Freed's Christmas extravaganzas at the Brooklyn Paramount; in Little Willie John's shake-'em-ups and Jackie Wilson's rope-a-dope at Harlem's legendary Apollo; in the guttural screams of early sixties Beatles 45s; and in the white-and-gold cape that Vegas Elvis wore from the late sixties until his untimely demise. It may be found as well in the power of the street vernacular of the poetics of Bob Dylan and in the swagger and muscle of Springsteen's four-hour concert marathons. It may be found in the out-of-this-world moonwalk of Motown Michael Jackson; in MC Hammer's

"Don't Hurt 'Em" sexercises; in P. Diddy's bravado-between-the-rap sheets; and in Usher's sob-in-the-throat musical hip-hop confessionals. It may be found in the crossover imitator Vanilla Ice and the tough-guy wannabes Boys II Men and *NSYNC. It may be found in the hard urban Whiteness of Eminem; the fem-dom smirk of the come-hither Madonna and the audaciously authentic antics of Pink. And it may be found in every urban back alley or country RFD, wherever and whenever young boys and girls sneak off in the night to kiss one another for the first time while the radio plays and their young hearts pulse to the reassuring beat of their own rhythmic love. It is true they may not know the words to the clarion love call of "Please Please Please," and they may not have even heard of the song from so long ago; nevertheless they live out its legacy in every moment of their hot, young, I'm-yours-forever passions.

There may no longer be any question that James Brown is a true American cultural icon, America's modern good-will ambassador whose smile is as instantly recognizable around the world as that of his predecessor, the late, great Louis Armstrong. There is a particular magic to the approach James Brown used, one of politeness that approached courtliness, in contrast to the intensity of his delivery. Two years after the initial success of "Please Please Please," James Brown recorded "Try Me," his twenty-first hit record in twenty-four months. Noting once again the extreme politeness of the song's voice, I asked him about that song, and this is what he told me: "'Try Me' was indicative of what I was attempting to accomplish in those days, to put my feelings in a way that I knew they needed to be. I knew I couldn't be too aggressive in front of mixed audiences, because they wouldn't accept me that way. So I consciously tried to put my songs in such a way their lyrics wouldn't offend. 'Try Me' is written in the context of a man trying to romance a woman, yes, but it's also talking to the White people in the audience. You've tried all the others—how about trying me? Meaning, how about giving my music and my show a chance? It was another way of saying please. That's what the song is really all about, pure and simple. I always wanted to be polite, even if I sounded forceful and confident when I sang. It was the key to my success, no matter how intense my performances got. It was no easy trick to maintain a certain way of writing a lyric while keeping the level of performing as intense as I could make it. I learned early on that the key to making it in show business, especially in the form of revue, was all in the presentation of whatever material you had."

The early James Brown Revue remains the stuff of legend. And as is the case with all legends, James Brown's real life is far more complex than his easily accessible, highly structured, courteous, and tunefully optimistic music might have led those audiences to believe. This was (and still is) a life made up of unequal parts fame and ignominy, spectacular success and crushing defeat, the glory of romance and the failure of love. Through his music he managed to bare his private soul, an act of expiation played out again and again for more than fifty years, in the central heat of the public's glorious, if unforgiving, spotlight. As with any creative and cultural force, it is often difficult, if not impossible, to sort out the foundations of that success; to accurately assess if, ultimately, it was his life that fed the music he produced or if it was the music that led him down the pathway of a life not always so well-lived.

As a first-rate songwriter, an entertainment figure of the highest rank, and a cultural force who has influenced the social order, James Brown has, as Dylan once noted about himself, already gone the distance. Offstage, however, his complex journey continues onward, as do his hard-fought battles to survive. To the horror of the eyebrow-arched (and almost exclusively White) "reporters" of the so-called entertainment press, those tabloid terrors who love nothing more than to convict and sentence any celebrities of color whenever "something *big*" (meaning "something *bad*") happens to them, without benefit of anything even approaching fairness and due process, James Brown has remained a longtime champion of all that he represents.

Really, how many times does one have to see the infamous 2004 mug shot where James Brown looks so scarily crazed? Did anyone, anywhere, ever bother to take the time to explain that it was taken by the police, after they came to his house in South Carolina and arrested him (following up on a domestic violence 911 call from his wife), at the tail end of the two-day blackout that had wiped out the East Coast in the summer of '03, and that he could not shower or even wash at the station, where what little water there was was being run by a generator, before he was made to stand in front of the unforgivingly sadistic "perp" lens? Did anyone, anywhere, ever bother to ask how or why that photo was released to the general public in time for the same-day late edition of every daily newspaper, local TV station, and scandal rag around the world? Who, besides the local police, the gossip hogs, and the old racist stereotypers, could possibly have found any pleasure or satisfaction, let alone justice, in that photo?

Certainly not James Brown's people—that is to say, not just his family and his friends, but his family of friends all around the world. To them, Black or White, Mr. Brown was most decidedly *not* the dangerous-looking loony in the photo, but rather the man he has been since the beginning of his career: a victim of aggressive racism tinged with jealousy, a universal symbol of American Black strength, pride, defiance, and survival.

For the worldwide generation of White boomers especially, who have in the past twenty years become his primary live audience, James Brown steadfastly remains the profound reflection of their own ongoing struggles for racial freedom and equality, peace, equal rights, color-blind democracy, and yes, the pursuit of love. In that sense, James Brown has, for half a century, sung lead on the collective soundtrack of their primal youth.

Today, at seventy-two years of age, James Brown, no matter in what external episode of chaos he finds himself— messy domestic situation, ongoing IRS problems, the irreversible reality of advancing age—can and still stands Black and proud and on his own two feet. He can and still does look out at every crowd he plays for with the pride of a man who has not just seen and done it all but lived to tell the tale. To him, every audience is Papa's brand-new bag, every performance as important as the first he ever gave, or the second, or the ten thousandth. It has to be that way, because to the person in the audience seeing him for the first time, it is the only performance that counts, and for James Brown, they're all just that important, one more cut on the soundtrack.

Much of the chronology of James Brown's life has become a permanent part of the legend. It begins May 3, 1933, with his first forward push into a world that didn't seem to want him in it at all. As would become his style for the rest of his life, the infant Brown quickly learned how to fight for his life. Pronounced stillborn by the attendant doctors, he was given virtually no chance of survival.

He somehow pulled through, ready to take his place among the numberless other poor and disenfranchised Blacks of the rural Depression South, where extreme poverty and constant upheaval were the only reward for making it past your first day on Earth.

When he was four years old, James Brown's mother, Susie, after a lot of arguing brought about by the difficult conditions of poverty and hopelessness they lived in, announced without any advance notice or warning that she was leaving her husband, Joe, and her young son for another, better-connected man. Joe begged her not to go. What about the boy? he asked, to which Susie replied with a coldness that could have frozen a summer lake, "You keep him."

It was a primal scene of rejection and disconsolation whose heat burned straight through to the boy's soul and singed it in a way that would never completely heal. "I wouldn't say it affected me," Mr. Brown said later, reflecting upon that first abandonment. "But rather it reminded me that no one ever feels your pain, the way your head aches and your heart breaks, quite the way you do, and because of it you really go through this world by yourself."

James Brown would not see his mother again for another twenty years. Joe and James moved to a shack in the woods, where the boy liked to keep to himself when daddy James was out looking for whatever work he might find. It was during these formative years that the isolated and lonely young James developed his raw-gut instinct for self-survival.

In 1938, at the age of five, young James was taken in by his aunt Honey and lived in her crowded house in the Augusta, Georgia, terry (short for what was then called by less tolerant minds the "Negro territory"). Her home was bursting with sixteen other discarded or unwanted children from her large, disjointed family. Aunt Honey's terry was rife with hookers, drugs, and moonshine—illegal, unstamped home-brew, enough to keep the soldiers stationed at nearby Daniel Field busy and happy during their off-base time. One of the first paying jobs young James had was hustling up soldiers to bring home to the house girls; he lived off the tips the soldiers gave him when they left.

There was something else about the terry that young James came to know well: the periodic marches undertaken by the white-sheeted, much-feared Klan. While the other, White kids who went to school learned to sing about sugar and spice, young James heard the tune sung Southern-style by the real boyz in the hood: *Sugar and spice and everything nice, Black man made for pig's feet and rice . . .*

It was scary and mean in the terry, but nothing young James saw there disturbed him as much as the fear visible in his father's eyes whenever he found time to visit—a fear that kept Joe Brown from standing up to the plentiful and ongoing abuse of the White man. When Joe was a young man, he served in the military, and often told James about seeing the White soldiers getting out of the front of the transport trains while the Blacks had to get out of the back, and that they even had two different color uniforms. As James Brown recalled years later, "He'd tell me how the Blacks all seemed invisible to the rest of the regulars, an image that the writer Ralph Ellison would later on use so powerfully in his great novel. According to his daddy, all Black men in America knew exactly what that felt like, being invisible to the sensitivities as well as separated from the privileges of the White man. Only when it came to taking a bullet and dying on the front was there any kind of equal opportunity."

It was something that took young James a lifetime to try to understand. Other immigrant races could, within a generation or two, pass into the mainstream because of the color of their skin. With Black people, that was impossible, because they wore the color of their heritage on their faces. There was never any way to hide the fact of being Black, even if one wanted to, which never even entered the equation of young James' youth.

So it was that whenever Joe came to Augusta to visit his son, no matter how badly Whitey treated him (and it was never what anybody could remotely call good), he always managed an acquiescent smile and a protective flurry of

yassirs and nawsirs. After, to vent his fury and humilia-
tion, he'd whup his own boy. Young James learned a hard
lesson through the pain of this acting out: a frightened
man is a cowed man, and a cowed man is a frightening
man. He promised himself before he was in long pants
that the only one he would ever fear in his life was the
good God Almighty Himself. Everybody else, no matter
what his color, but especially Whitey, had better know
how to fight if he wanted to try to take a piece of James
Brown.

A couple of early incidents were burned into James'
memory so hot and deep the scars would never completely
heal. One day young James was working in the fields and a
couple of White guys thought it might be fun to try to
electrocute him by forcing him to cut into a live wire while
dousing him with water. He somehow managed to survive
that, but from then on made it a point to try to steer clear
of the Southern White Man as much as possible.

It wasn't always possible. Another time James had to
deal with some crazy local White ex-GI who often liked to
boast to his buddies over drinks about the steel plate in his
head that he received thanks to combat, and about the
civilian R & R he enjoyed: tying young Black kids to trees
to watch them scream and beg in order to, as he put it,
"break their spirit." When he grabbed young James and began to lash him to a big oak, the boy did not resist or com-

plain and stayed tied to the tree for hours until the man realized he wasn't going to get a fear show and, bored with waiting, finally let him go. The next day James looked for the man, found him in the street outside the bar, and without saying a word walked up to him, hit him over the head with an empty glass bottle, and left him stretched out cold on the pavement. The man never bothered him or any young Black boy from the terry again.

The one positive thing James did get out of his childhood was a love of music, and an early awareness that he had a natural ability to make it. He could play the harmonica at five, without ever taking a single music lesson (he still can't read music). When he was seven, young James got a job working as a delivery boy for the local liquor store. There he met another boy, Leon Austin, who taught him how to play a little piano. After hours of endless repetition spent mastering the three-chord progression for the right hand and the simultaneous, accompanying bass line for the left, young James developed into an accomplished keyboardist, routinely working out the relatively intricate finger parts of such favorite boogie songs of his as "Coonshine Baby."

At about the same time he picked up the finger-and-chord basics of blues guitar from "Tampa Red" (Hudson Whitaker), a local brothel entertainer who worked at Aunt Honey's, and who happened to be dating one of her daughters. "Tampa Red" showed James how to play trad blues in an open-chord tuning with a bottleneck slide.

And there was always the radio, where, among the endless redneck country music stations that clotted the dial and said nothing to young James, he first discovered the skip-wave stations of the North that offered the pop tune stylings of Bing Crosby and Frank Sinatra and the piano sounds of the one and only Count Basie. Sometimes, if the DJ on these stations liked the record, he'd play it over and over again, just as if he were sitting in his living room, getting into it, letting it get into him. And young James went for it in a big way.

Finally, it was gospel music that completed the picture. Gospel music, even more than the Good Book itself, was what kept James coming back to the local Baptist houses of worship. There was one preacher young James Brown particularly loved, the traveling Bishop "Daddy" Grace and his House of Prayer. In the late forties and early fifties, Grace was hugely popular among poor Black Southern folk because he offered the best Sunday music around. Sporting long curly hair and glistening fingernails, "Daddy" dressed lavishly and always wore a cape, something young James Brown couldn't get over. Grace would talk/sing his sermons, using melody to emphasize his words as he worked his congregation into a frenzy. He even added drums to his church sets, something that the first time young James heard them grabbed him by the ears and yanked him up straight.

After that, the boy keyed into the majesty, the music, and the magic that is at the heart of all good gospel preaching, and how "the scream," as he would later call it, was the ultimate expression of spiritual rather than physical pain. It was this cry of the pain of the oppressed, those forced to drink from the other water fountain, that would, through James Brown, one day become the cry of liberation.

So inspired by Grace was young James that at the age of twelve he formed his own gospel group. He called it the Cremona Trio, quickly adding the music of Black jazz and his favorite bebop man, Louis Jordan, especially the celebrated "Caldonia," to the show.

James Brown's schooling ended when he was ten. He had barely gained enough education at Silas X. Ford School to learn to read a little and write some, his studies supplemented at night by Aunt Honey, who practiced reading with him by taking him through the comics—the "funny books," as she called them. For the sake of survival itself, young James had to go to work all day in Georgia's blistering cotton fields, sometimes picking cotton, sometimes cutting red sugarcane, occasionally picking peanuts. The rent for Aunt Honey's house was up to five dollars a month and she couldn't make it without his help.

To earn extra money, at night after work in the fields, James set up shop on the sidewalks of Augusta outside the entrance to the local radio station WRDW with his

shoeshine kit and offered his services to the passing soldiers. To attract them to his box and away from the others
that dotted Main Street, young James would buck dance
for the soldiers, who, to show their appreciation, always
threw him a couple of extra pennies, maybe three cents,
sometimes a nickel if he danced real nice. To stretch his
take even more, before going home, and after the last soldier had disappeared from the streets, young James would
search through the corner garbage cans for anything that
might be edible that the rats hadn't already gotten their
teeth into.

Thirty years later he would own WRDW.

By working day and night, through sheer ambition and a
bit of charm and talent, James managed to earn his age
every week, while old Joe had never manage to earn more
than seven dollars a week his entire life. This said something to James, although he wasn't as yet exactly sure what
it was he was hearing.

Working the hot fields and mean streets of Augusta
fried James like a cheap burger, one side young and ten-
der, the other rough and tough. He didn't think he was big
enough. He didn't think he was smart enough. He didn't
think he was good-looking enough, at least not in the eyes
of the men and women who were in charge of everything.
Like most Blacks, he thought that all White people were
rich and superior and would forever call the shots. Even
as he learned how to buck and smile for Redneck Whitey,

the Black chip on his shoulder turned into a hot boulder, and soon rebellion won out over compliance and the young would-be tough-kid thug found himself in serious trouble.

It happened when he started going after what he wanted but without wanting to pay. He had the transported anger of a boy humiliated first at school and then on the streets for his ragamuffin look. To make sure that he would never suffer such an indignity again, he began stealing clothes from the nearby retail stores. Pretty soon he joined a local gang with his best friend, Thomas Cook, and was given the first of his many nicknames—Little Junior—and with the others began stealing whatever was available, expanding their inventory from threads to the contents of unlocked parked cars along Broad Street, often plucking the hubcaps off the vehicles as well. To Little Junior's way of thinking, people rich enough to own a car owed it to the poor people to do a little sharing. That made him less a thief than a Robin Hood, he told himself when he and the others divided their take.

The local judge didn't quite see it or him that way. In 1949, at the age of sixteen, James was arrested, convicted of petty and repeated theft, and sent up for a 3.5-year stretch at Alto Reform School in Toccoa, Georgia. Young James didn't understand why he was put away—they wouldn't send him to school for free, but they were willing to lock him up. *Crazy.*

Juvey was unrelenting Hell for James, until he rediscovered his connection to the church there, via what was for him the always compelling allure of gospel music, this time coming from the prison church, where he was soon playing it for the other boys. Before long he started another gospel singing group and was so good he acquired from the other inmates his next nickname, Music Box, the boy who could sing and also dance like none of the others. Music Box couldn't help but notice how the girls across the way on the women's side dug him for his singing and his moves.

While incarcerated, he also discovered, when he began to train as a boxer during his off hours, that he had an athletic ability well beyond his compact 5'6", 137-pound frame. He quickly became a formidable opponent in his weight class. One of his homeboy heroes had been Bo Jack, lightweight champion of the world, who had grown up on the same mean streets of Augusta, Georgia. Now young James molded his fighting style after Jack's, and in doing so developed a reputation as a fierce slugger—that is, until one afternoon in the ring when he was caught by a hard right hand that knocked him flat on his rear. After that, he turned his attention to baseball.

He was good enough at this sport as well to think about maybe one day pitching in the Black leagues until that dream was cut short by an injury to his knee ending any chance of him making it in professional sports. Now he decided that when he got out, music was *it*.

He shared his goals with the parole board, who freed him after he'd written them a letter stating his intention saying that if he were released he wanted to devote his life "to singing for the Lord." What convinced them even more than the letter was a visit by a local gospel singer, Bobby Byrd, who had heard about the boy everyone was talking about, come to the reform school to check him out, and wound up telling the board he was willing to sponsor young James' singing career on the outside.

Shortly after his eighteenth birthday, James Brown was released from Alto and became a member of Bobby Byrd's Ever Ready Gospel Singers, a Georgia-based vocal quartet that at the time just so happened to be looking to widen its focus from God's music to rhythm and blues. Most groups made their hometown part of their name and, because of doing so, remained forever local. One night local R & B star Little Richard happened to hear the group and urged Byrd to expand their reach beyond the terry, up to Macon, Richard's home base. To emphasize the significance of the move, Byrd changed the name of his group to the more secular, some might say devilish, the Flames, purposely leaving out any geographical reference so no one would quite know where he and the other boys were actually from. Nowhere, in show business, Richard explained to Byrd, meant everywhere.

By the mid-fifties, the band had become James Brown and the Famous Flames, featuring James Brown as its lead singer. The self-proclaimed "Napoléon of the stage," the one they talked about with the nitroglycerin in his pants, had quickly built a small but intense following in the Black bars and clubs of Macon, Georgia. It was a deliberate course he was following, his goal to "make it," to "be somebody," so that nothing and nobody would ever be able to put him away again, to take away the name that belonged to him, James Brown, and exchange it for a number on the back of his shirt.

One night, while performing, the Famous Flames were spotted by talent scout Ralph Bass of the Federal label, a subsidiary of the well-known Southern-based independent King Records, which was owned and operated by the already legendary Syd Nathan. Bass liked what he saw and soon negotiations began to sign the group. On February 4, 1956, James Brown and the Famous Flames recorded their first single, a James Brown original, "Please Please Please" (backed with "Why Do You Do Me?" on the flip side), at the famed R & B King/Federal studios in Cincinnati, Ohio. "Please Please Please" was released later that same month, the same week that Presley's groundbreaking "Hound Dog" came out on RCA. Even as Elvis dominated White rock and roll, James Brown and the Famous Flames' single shot to #5 on the R & B charts.

Among the many accomplishments of "Please Please Please" was its ability to strengthen R & B's commercial appeal by deepening the sound with a little bit of soul. In

James Brown's words: "'Please Please Please' was recorded in a small studio on a cheap ten-cent mike, the glorious Shure microphone I used before all the high technology came along and 'cleaned up' the great sound of fifties music—the same cheap mike that Elvis used for all his Sun recordings. 'Please Please Please' made it possible for us and other Black performers to move away from the soft, smooth, and for the most part desexualized sound of harmonious Black doo-wop and easy-listening club music that had gained some appeal with the White, record-buying audience, into a more muscular, directly gospel-rooted sound that invigorated the beat, that in turn enabled us to release the heat."

"Please Please Please" quickly became James Brown's signature song, its presentation a complete mini-melodrama as profoundly rendered as anything previously seen on any nightclub stage or at any Southern Baptist church. In it, James Brown sang of the special burning pain of lost love, and when he dropped to his knees to beg his woman to come back, this nightly death-by-heartbreak, a tightly choreographed operetta of unbridled emotion, complete with purple spotlight, glittering cape, and commiserating assistant, Danny Ray, he drove audiences into a frenzy. After the arrival of "Please Please Please," nothing about the sound, the look, the emotion, and the culture of modern American Black music would ever be the same.

A year later, increasingly at odds with Syd Nathan for his refusal to allow him to record with the actual members of the Flames (Nathan preferred pickup musicians in the studio to save money, his reasoning being that if you couldn't see them it didn't make any difference who was playing), James Brown quit the label, changed the name of the band to Nat Kendrick and the Swans, and recorded a song that would eventually put them back on the charts: his self-financed instrumental recording of "(Do the) Mashed Potatoes."

Thus encouraged, James Brown launched a solo career assault on soul-tinged R & B and, having made his point, returned to King Records and Syd Nathan. Their reunion produced the spectacular "Try Me," another song that Nathan had no faith in, so much so that James was forced to pay for the recording out of his own pocket. Upon its release "Try Me" exploded onto the charts at #1, went on to become the biggest selling R & B chart single of 1958. "Try Me" initiated an incredible run of seventeen James Brown chart toppers.

By 1959, James Brown's only significant rival was Little Richard, who had managed to do the one thing that, with the exception of Chuck Berry and Fats Domino, none of the other hard Black performers of the day could: make a dent in the White pop charts. A new rivalry between Little Richard and James Brown developed on the Southern Chitlin club circuit so deep that Richard was afraid to run into James Brown offstage, believing if he did he would get his face punched in, which he might well have. The rivalry took many forms, including the way they dressed for the stage. A lot of what later became the signature James Brown garb may be traced to his early years in which he tried to outdo the always flamboyant Little Richard.

During his years on the Chitlin Circuit, James Brown kept a detailed record of which Southern promoters wouldn't book him on an integrated card. He was always made to play the "Colored" show houses, eat in the "Colored" restaurants, go to the "Colored" bathrooms, and stay in the "Colored" hotels. To dress for these shows, he had to use the backseat of his own car, because no decent dressing rooms were provided for the "Colored" acts, even in their best theaters. More than once the James Brown Revue—as the act was now being called—was referred to by White promoters as "that bunch of niggers." White stage managers, too, called them "those niggers" as they cued the band onto the stage to the screams of joy from the mixed audience audiences sending all that love up to them. It was something the other Black acts took as the price of performing in the South, but not James Brown. He remembered each and every one of those promoters, and later on, when he became the Godfather of Soul, he refused to allow any of them to book his shows. That, he would tell them, was *his* price for being a performer in the South.

According to James Brown, "At the time I knew I had to stay in my place, and was grateful to have a place, as difficult and racist as it was, in order to work. Because of it, I had to impose very strict behavior on the other Flames. Among other things, I didn't want a slip of someone's tongue to get him, and me, killed. That's when I first decided that everyone, including me, had to be addressed by Mr. or Mrs. and their last name. Internal regimentation was not just a safer way to live, but the only way. Politeness, I knew, was the only guarantee that we would survive the toughest of venues and get to live another day."

This was no exaggeration. More than once, Mr. Brown's life was threatened for the smallest things that were said among the band members, over which he had no control. And when things came to a head, he knew that if he so much as opened his mouth there were plenty of White men more than ready to enjoy the sport of killing him. As a result, Mr. Brown chose men who could fight to work in his Revue. They could and did save his life in confrontations brought about first by careless words, and later on by nothing so much as the fact that here he was, a Black man, flying around in a private plane, all the excuse needed to fan the bloodthirsty rage (and jealousy) of Southern redneck racists who were forever trouble bound. The presence of muscle, Mr. Brown knew, was always going to be his best defense, because as no one knew better than he did: "In those days you didn't dare to confront them directly, because it meant someone was going to die and that someone was likely to have dark skin."

In October 1962, having survived the lawless Wild West feel of the Chitlin Circuit, the James Brown Revue took a major step up in the world when it was booked to play the world-famous Apollo in New York, the apotheosis of American Black popular entertainment.

On the program besides the James Brown Revue were some of the greatest names in R & B, including Solomon Burke, Freddie King, the Valentinos, and comedian Pigmeat Markham. The highlight of the run was a live midnight recording of the show made on October 24, 1962, funded by Brown himself, based on the phenomenally successful 1960 Ray Charles live concert recording *Ray Charles in Person*.

Brown financed the making of the album because Nathan refused to, insisting that regardless of the Ray Charles recording, he didn't think anyone would buy a live version of a song they already owned on a studio-produced album. Brown knew better, went ahead and invested every cent he had or could get his hands on, all of $5,700, and gave the performance of his life that night. By the time the curtain came down he was seven pounds lighter.

Upon its release (owned by James Brown, distributed by King), *James Brown: Live at the Apollo* sold one million

copies, a number previously unheard of for an R & B performance album. The simple fact was, no one had ever
heard anything like it before. It stayed on the charts for an
astonishing sixty-six weeks, a run that once and for all confirmed James Brown as the biggest Black American R & B
star.

One of the first things the success of the album did was
deliver to Mr. Brown the means to step up to the role of
R & B's modern-day savior. He vowed to lead his people
out of the wilderness of pervasive record-industry exploita-
tion, which endlessly and brazenly ripped off young Black
artists. He began by instituting a lawsuit close to home,
against Syd Nathan and King Records, to regain what he
believed was the rightful ownership of all his previous
masters (original recordings). It would prove a long, difficult, and expensive suit, but in the end, after years of legal
battles, he succeeded in winning the future rights to the
music that he had written and that he had inadvertently
handed over to Mr. Nathan's company. By being able to
determine the fate of his masters, James Brown finally become the master of his fate.

The next thing he did was to make the epic move out of
Georgia to the musical mecca that was the New York City
of the sixties. He gave the house he had bought for himself in Macon to Joe, and bought a new one for himself, a
twelve-room Victorian house in Queens, New York City,

directly from Cootie Williams, Duke Ellington's legendary trumpet player, for the then enormous sum of ten thousand dollars. James Brown paid for it in cash.

He then reinvested much of what remained of his new-found wealth in the Black ghetto communities of America. He opened a successful string of Gold Platter soul food restaurants, and began putting together a conglomerate to purchase several regional radio stations. The idea was to promote, by example, the image of the self-made and therefore self-owned Black man. By doing so, he hoped to provide tangible inspiration to a generation of Blacks that would show them they could make it in the White man's world without fear of automatically being exploited and ripped off.

On his own radio stations, he carefully programmed Black *and* White music on the same shows, to avoid being labeled a promoter of only "race music" and therefore guilty of reverse racism. He always played a lot of Frank Sinatra for no other reason than he loved the way the cat sang. "Saturday Night Is the Loneliest Night of the Week" was one Mr. Brown's special favorites, and later on, "My Way" sounded to him as near to an anthem to romantic as well as of artistic independence as anything he had ever heard before. That song, Mr. Brown thought, was being sung directly to him, because he, too, had done it his way.

Being in the business of radio was one of the best ways

he found he could continue to better himself, both personally and professionally, to show by example that both could be done successfully by a Black man in America. James Brown explains it this way: "I had reached a point of success where I knew I was through forever fattening frogs for the snakes. I was now in a place where I had the opportunity to do things for myself. Before I got there, I, meaning we, meaning Black people, was not allowed to get it any other way than serving the White man in America."

All of his accomplishments notwithstanding, James Brown was still categorized by the mainstream music critics as a "Black" performer, whose music was intended for, and largely heard and seen by, Black kids, on Black radio stations, in the purple neon clubs that dotted the South, and the Black sections of the cities of the North. It wasn't until 1964 that all of that irrevocably changed, when James Brown was booked to appear on a theater-only closed-circuit industry show beamed out of the Santa Monica Civic Auditorium. The show was shot on kinescope for possible later release as a feature or television film.

What was unique about it was the unusually high mix of Black and White acts, a kind of extension of the sort of variety shows Ed Sullivan had been doing on television for years, using rock and roll as the umbrella under which he presented Elvis Presley, the Supremes, and Bo Diddley, among many other chart toppers. Scheduled to appear with the White acts—the still relatively unknown Rolling Stones, local surf rock gods Jan and Dean, British Invasion idols Gerry and the Pacemakers, and protofeminist rocker Lesley Gore—were such notable Black acts as Chuck Berry, Bo Diddley, the Supremes, Smokey Robinson and the Miracles, and Marvin Gaye.

In what is universally regarded as the most astonishing performance in the entire history of rock and roll, Mr. Brown's twenty-minute rendition of "Please Please Please" not only tore the house down—it nearly wrecked Mick Jagger and the other Stones. Like everyone else at the Santa Monica Civic that night (and anyone who has ever seen the kinescope), the Stones recognized the obvious as it was happening: no band, they learned, not even one as intense as the early, raw, still-bluesy Stones, could *ever* follow James Brown. The warm November night marked James Brown's official crossover into the White mainstream via his unique style of *rock-a-soul*, a night in which he changed forever the face and course of popular music, and the teen culture that looked to it for its anthemic identity.

Even as James Brown was busy stretching the acceptable boundaries of "race" music in America, the nation itself was being ripped apart. These were the early, violent years of the sixties, the first years of the American expansion into Vietnam, the nascent flowering of the boomer-driven civil rights movement. While young African-Americans were being shot dead in the streets or routinely lynched from the tallest trees in Tennessee, Mississippi, and Alabama, their White brothers and sisters from the North were coming of age, and racial equality was their clarion call. The boomers had been set up for battle while still in knee pants, thanks to the 1954 Supreme Court decision Brown *v*. Board of Education of Topeka, and first let their teenage hair down during the brief but unforgettable era of JFK's Camelot, a youth-oriented, forward-looking thousand days creatively highlighted by the crossover successes of singer Harry Belafonte, actor Sidney Poitier, and jazz trumpeter Miles Davis, and historically by the daring actions of the Northern-based Freedom Riders, which culminated in the horrifying slaughter of Schwerner, Chaney, and Goodman. Turmoil marched alongside progress through the dark days, with the murders of Emmett Till, Medgar Evers, and JFK himself, the signing of the Civil Rights Act of 1964, the rise of the Reverend Dr. Martin Luther King Jr., the March on Washington, the heavyweight championship of Muhammad Ali, and the separatist policies of Malcolm X, all accompanied by the pop-flavored R & B of Detroit's Motown, Memphis' Stax, and as always, soul brother number one, the ultra-independent James Brown.

Rock-a-soul became the universal cultural link for boomers of all races on the streets and campuses across the country when, in 1965, the civil rights movement united with the growing youth protest against the War in Vietnam. That same year James Brown released what would become his epochal signature song, "Papa's Got a Brand New Bag."

That song released a cultural tsunami with its celebrated but often misunderstood "One," the rhythm that gave the civil rights and peace movements their definitive marching beat. The "One" changed everything, from the definition of pride to the implication of what it meant to walk—on the "One"—like a man. Indeed, with the "One," James Brown had thrown out all the traditional chord progressions along with his sweet melodies, the salad *and* the dressing of R & B and soul—and retained only the thick juicy cut of the rhythm. Gone along with the excess was the timidity, the apologetic head-down shuffle of Black musical passivity. James Brown's "One" represented pride and authority, a sound that stepped up to the mike with strength and conviction, and a generation of Black and White boomers instantly embraced it *on the good foot*.

"Papa's Got a Brand New Bag" proved as crucial to the social and cultural zeitgeist of the sixties as Dylan's "Like a Rolling Stone" and the Stones' "Satisfaction," all three of which were released in 1965, the decade's pivotal musical year. "Papa's Got a Brand New Bag" not only topped the R & B charts for eight weeks, but more significantly, for the first time a James Brown single appeared on the White pop charts, making its entrance in typically grand style by breaking and entering into the Top Ten, a triumph he would follow up with more pop chart hits—*ninety-six*—more than the Stones, more than the Beatles, more than any other artist in Billboard's history, except Elvis Presley.

On Friday night, April 5, 1968, James Brown was scheduled to perform at the fourteen-thousand-seat packed-to-the-rafters Boston Garden. Everything was in place until the afternoon before, when America, with the seeming regularity of a recurring nightmare, once more erupted into race-rooted violence with the shocking assassination of the Reverend Dr. Martin Luther King Jr. As the news of his murder in Memphis spread, Boston, like several other cities in America with a strong, if cordoned-off, Black ghetto, was threatening to erupt in flames, a blaze that could crisscross the country and easily turn America into an inferno of rage. For his own safety and that of his fans, James Brown considered canceling his show. But he decided to go through with it after Mayor Kevin White arranged to have it broadcast live.

Facing a packed house that could have easily passed for an extremely angry teenage mob ready to explode into a full-scale riot, James Brown single-handedly calmed the kids down by going up to the mike and promising an evening of great music dedicated to the memory of the fallen leader. His intention was to serve as a symbolic conduit of peace and stability for an uneasy audience, and nation, reeling from years of unchecked political assassination and the ravages of an unwinnable war in Vietnam. That memorable night, his message to "build it, don't burn it" became a cornerstone of the sixties boomer vernacular.

As the sixties morphed into the seventies, James Brown's ostentatious outfits, considered by many to be more "Sammy" than "soul," his processed 'do, and his whole show began to seem less gutsy than glitzy. By the end of the seventies, Mr. Brown was still considered at the top of his game, having sold an astonishing eighty-three million records, and keeping more than eight hundred songs in his performing repertoire. Yet changing tastes in music and shifting political winds had crept in and taken their toll on his career and life.

A growing faction of next-generation young Blacks felt that Mr. Brown's politics—he had, after all, enthusiastically supported both Humphrey *and* Nixon—sent the wrong message to America's Black youth, and that he should have been more outspoken against a war that had sent far more of his own people to Vietnam to die than "Whitey's." And in the wake of hit factories Earth, Wind & Fire, Bloodstone, War, and other more "hip" Black groups, James Brown was unceremoniously being relegated to the rear of a Black generation's social conscience.

Undaunted by the changing social tastes, he stood by his credo, one that had served him well throughout his life. "You have to know the pros and the cons of where you're going, what you're doing, and what's going to happen when you don't. Then, don't get mad, don't get angry, get smart." He maintained his patriotic stance in his shows, took time off to tour Africa, voluntarily entertained troops in Vietnam (without the cooperation, encouragement, or funding of the U.S. government, but with the extensive behind-the-scenes help of Bob Hope, who talked to President Johnson and encouraged him to let James Brown go to Vietnam to entertain "his own kind"), and encouraged urban ghetto youth to continue to build rather than burn.

Nevertheless, because he consistently refused to change his tune, for all his work in the name of social progress, James Brown was loudly accused by several in the Black community of "Uncle Tomning." Shockingly, by the end of the seventies he was considered by a growing part of the Black community to be as much a part of the nation's stalled racial progress as of its solution.

Still he pressed on. In 1986, James Brown was formally inducted into the Rock and Roll Hall of Fame, and after too long an absence, he returned to the pop charts with the single "Living In America" from *Rocky IV*, a song that he performed in the movie (and a song, by the way, as much misinterpreted as Bruce Springsteen's "Born in the USA").

Nevertheless, despite the official accolades and the occasional hit single, the hard truth was, he was less in demand than at any time since the days before "Please Please Please." As the eighties wound down, out of the mainstream and off the charts, James Brown let his frustration turn to self-destruction, manifested in domestic problems, serious addictions, and increasing fits of unexplainable (and uncontrollable) violence. By 1988, both Mr. Brown and his third wife, Adrianne, were addicted to PCP. On September 24, an enraged Mr. Brown burst into his own office and angrily accused his forty-person staff of using his private bathroom without permission. When his mood turned violent, the police were called. Mr. Brown ran, but was quickly apprehended. He was tried and sentenced to six years' hard time in the big house for aggravated assault, fleeing the scene of a crime, and failure to obey police orders to surrender.

James Brown had hit bottom.

He wound up serving 2.5 years before being paroled. Released on February 27, 1991, he wasted no time working to rehabilitate his own name and reputation, to recapture the two things he felt were most worthy of salvation—his music and his soul. He went back on the road and was shocked and gratified by how warmly audiences all over the world embraced him and encouraged his return to the stage, signaling one of the greatest comebacks in the history of music.

A year later, during an emotional evening at the 34th

Annual Grammy Ceremonies, the audience, filled with veterans of the music industry and the new kids in town, many of whom were born after the release of "Please Please Please," stood as one to cheer James Brown as he was given a Lifetime Achievement Award for his great body of music, for his ongoing fight for civil rights, for his unwavering patriotism, and for his hard-earned spiritual redemption.

On December 7, 2003, he was awarded one of the coveted Kennedy Center Honors for the performing arts. The night of the ceremonies, he sat alongside fellow recipients Carol Burnett, Loretta Lynn, Mike Nichols, and Itzhak Perlman, and when his name was called, he listened as the nation paid tribute to the man who gave rhythm and blues its soul, and who then reinvented both himself and his music into funk, while elevating the self-image of his people.

He was introduced that night by Blues Brother Dan Ackroyd, and presented with his award by no less a figure of Black prominence than Colin Powell, the U.S. Secretary of State, who called James Brown "America's secretary of soul and its foreign minister of funk." As the Kennedy Center thundered with applause, a tearful James Brown held his head high and nodded humbly to the gathering, proud of all that he had done, and all that he had become. In 2003, James Brown proved it by making an

emotional return to the Apollo Theater for a landmark series of concerts he called Seven Decades of Funk.

H ere, then, is the *real* story of James Brown, told by the
Godfather of Soul himself, what he calls his "personal
business" rather than his "show business," the real 411 of
his life, an interior monologue whose essential roots are
not just about music but about race, whose obsession is
not inclusion but exclusion, whose ultimate resolution oc-
curs not onstage but within the heart . . . and from the
soul.

With all his complexities, idiosyncrasies, extraordinary
abilities, and ruthless demons, with all his unbelievable
strengths and talents, and all his debilitating weaknesses,
James Brown remains what he has been for more than fifty
years—an American master—and as such, a major con-
tributor to the culture of his time and ours, a poet of the
first rank, and an entertainer without equal. It is in that
spirit that I introduce you to my friend Mr. James Brown.

I FEEL GOOD

ONE

A T THE AGE OF SEVENTY, FEELING NO MORE THAN thirty-five on a bad day, I returned to the Apollo Theater for two nights in November 2003 to celebrate the fortieth anniversary of the recording and subsequent release of *James Brown: Live at the Apollo,* an album that changed my life, and the business I'm in of bringing popular music to the masses.

I've always thought of the Apollo as the big judge. Before you get there, up until the first time you are privileged enough to take the stage, you're on probation. You haven't done hard time in the business, but you qualify to play the Big House. After you've performed on the legendary stage, and lived to tell the tale, you are on what I call parole. You been there, you done it, you're free at last.

I had called this latest edition of my Revue Seven Decades of Funk, and as I had hoped, it proved to be one of the greatest triumphs of my career. I'd lost weight, I was in fighting-style thin and trim, my face was not as hard-looking or as bloated as it had been in recent years, my mustache was gone, my voice was stronger, and I still had what some call charisma—and what I call soul. I mean, brother, I was *ready* and I was *there.*

The Revue was tight, well-oiled, and intact, similar to the type of show that I had first started presenting some fifty years earlier—and as it had back then it still left the audiences in awe. I was *outta sight!* It was like a ride in a time machine. No one could quite figure out how I still did it, from my acrobatic splits to the quality of my singing. That's what made the show magical, for the audience as well as for me.

I like to think of my many years as an entertainer in intervals of time, highlighted along the way by certain individual moments of particularly deep and personal meaning. The night in October 1962, for example, that I recorded *Live at the Apollo* certainly qualifies as one of the most satisfying of those. I suppose a fair amount, but not all of it, has to do with money. I completely self-financed that record at a cost of $5,700, which was every bit of coin I could lay my hands on at the time. It was more than a financial bet—it was the greatest career risk I or anyone I knew had ever taken. Today, of course, it would cost hundreds of thousands of dollars to make the album the way I did it back then, but at the time that $5,700 felt to me like $57 million. The thing was, I knew enough about life by then to know that the hardest accomplishment is always the first, like that first baby step you take down your long walk through life. I wanted to show people who had never seen me what my live shows were all about, what they were missing if they had never experienced James Brown "live," so that they would then want to see and hear even more of James Brown.

It might surprise you to know that *Apollo* was the first live album recorded with no separation of tracks. All the songs run together just like they did in the show, with no space between the grooves. I did that on purpose, to make sure the listening experience was closer to the actual live performance than any other album had so far. It also made it impossible to release any of the cuts as a single. To me, the value of the album was as much in the protection of the music as a creative whole as it was as a financial product. If people could buy pieces of it, why would they buy the whole thing? My intention was to deliver a complete show, not just the coming attractions. I wanted people to experience the whole show via this album as close to the way it happened as I could make it.

I thank God that we accomplished what we set out to do. The success of that album and all that came from it became a testament on vinyl and later on CD to something amazing that took place that night, nothing less than a spiritual connection, a midnight gospel between me and my audience with all the blues and funk and soul that I had inside.

Of course, the triumph of that night was really a kind of an illusion, because concert audiences always fantasize they're getting more than they actually are. Like with everything else in America, we always imagine and hope that we are getting more for our dollar than we are actually willing to pay for. When people see the James Brown Revue, and then compare it to other shows they've seen, not necessarily just the older acts but the new, younger ones as well, they believe they are seeing the difference between what is possible and what is not in the music industry. They see what can be done, what *needs* to be done, and what *should* be done—and then they fill in the corners and the gaps so that they are able to imagine an even greater spectacle has taken place than the one they are already getting. In fact, I have more people onstage than I really need, so many that I could significantly pare down the presentation and nobody would ever really know the difference. The trick is, the audience has no idea where the fat is and where the lean is, and I certainly am not going to tell them! Is it those trombones, the baritones, that electric bass instead of the traditional upright? The bottom line is, if I had to, I could go onstage solo, with only a keyboard and microphone and nothing else and still put on a kick-ass show and no one would think for a second they were missing anything. I know, because I've done it!

However, I am proud to say that whether it's been a one-man show or a Revue of dozens, I've always put on a first-class performance, never cutting any corners to save a dollar if it meant taking anything away from the performance quality.

This time around, in November 2003, I decided to once again record the show, using the latest equipment and technology. I have to say that the results were impressive. The ghosts of the Apollo's sacred past were all in attendance that night. Just as I can hear the magic on the '62 recording, I can hear it today, as well. After so many years in decline, that glorious theater had been refurbished and given some sort of soul transplant. My return, then, signified a triumph for the theater as much as it did for me.

Very few venues are big enough to contain me and my music, and to give both a certain pedigree by virtue of the spirits that inhabit the seats and the boxes the way the magical stage of the Apollo can.

Through the years, it has been gratifying for me to see all the stars who have passed through the great theater's hallowed passageway and who along the way have adapted various elements of my own stage and performance style. I was the first to do things a certain way before anyone else—like the Revue form of my shows. Unlike most shows at the time, I didn't just come out, sing, take a bow, and leave. I wanted to present an evening of James Brown—his songs, his friends, his instruments, his women, and his soul. And to do it with all the lighting, pinspots, sharp clothes, and atomic energy I had within me.

Others may have followed in my wake, but I was the one who turned racist minstrelsy into Black soul—and by doing so, became a cultural force. I both appreciate and am humbled by it.

I was a pioneer in a business sense as well. In my early days, the price of admission to the Apollo was ninety-nine cents. Based on the popularity of my shows, I was able to raise it three dollars to cover the expense of putting on a Revue like mine. I knew it was a risk, and that I was putting the onus on myself to justify that kind of money. What's more, I was the first performer to come up with the idea of renting out the theater and working for myself rather than the Man. When I saw how much the owners of the Apollo were taking in from all the shows they were able to squeeze out of us in a single day—sometimes as many as ten—and how little we, the performers, were making from the box-office take, I decided to simply rent the theater out for a week, pay all the operating expenses, and keep what was left for myself. Again, it took every dime I had to follow through on my convictions and do what they call "four-walling"—paying to rent the venue and doing whatever I wanted with it. That meant I was responsible for everything from selling the popcorn and paying the electric bills to filling the seats. It was a tremendous risk, but I had to do it.

At the end of the first week, my manager at the time, Mr. Syd Nathan, who was the owner of King Records, as well as my producer, was clearly worried. This was nothing new—worrying was Mr. Nathan's religion. But we hadn't sold out every seat, not even close, and I still had to pay everybody no matter how much or how little we took in. By the time the last show of the Revue's run was finished, we barely had a thousand dollars left over. But that didn't bother me as much as it did Mr. Nathan. I enjoyed the experience so much that I vowed to do it again the exact same way the next time I played the theater. Sure enough, when we returned a few months later, I four-walled the place again and this time we sold out every seat. There were lines around the block two and three people wide, and by the end of that week we had made ourselves a pretty penny.

Four-walling became my way of producing my own shows. The adventure of the risk was as great as the thrill of the reward. Once it became profitable, everybody did it, and it soon became a standard way of doing business in the world of entertainment. Today, stars like Clint Eastwood and Sylvester Stallone now routinely finance their own productions so that they can actually make some money for all their hard work. It was one of the reasons performers like James Arness stayed on *Gunsmoke* for twenty years. Believe me, he didn't do it simply because he liked riding horses! The network had done a smart thing—they had made him the producer of his own show. As long as somebody made money, everybody made money, and I believe that kept the show and Arness on the air for two successful decades.

It's the same in any organized situation—the one in power is the one who makes the money, and the one who makes the most money is the one who is working for himself. It's a philosophy I've employed since my earliest days performing at the Apollo, both for the live album and for my four-wall engagements. The lessons I learned from it were simple, but not those you might expect. Rich is not the lesson, by the way. *Power* is. Can you see that?

When Black entertainers in the fifties and sixties followed my lead and were able to gain a measure of financial clout, it was seen as the acquisition of power in the community of our culture—and at the same time as a threat to the mainstream status quo. Whenever we stood tall and sang without apology, the authorities wouldn't stand for it.

In many ways, the entire civil rights movement began when a White kid in the audience stood up and cheered for a Black performer. The great fear was that if a White man's teenage daughter saw James Brown perform onstage one night, the next night she'd be in his bed. And that was something that the mainstream wouldn't stand for. Any display of sexuality on our part was taken as a criminal threat. And the only retaliation the authorities had was to throw us in jail. They didn't like it when Chuck Berry did it, they didn't like it when Ray Charles did it, they didn't like it when Little Willie John did it, and at one time or another, they locked all of them up, including me.

God Almighty but I loved Little Willie, who, sadly, died in the penitentiary. Let me tell you about it

The first time I played the Apollo, in April of 1959, Little Willie was the headliner. He was riding high on a string of hit singles, "All Around the World," "Let Them Talk," "Talk to Me," and of course, "Fever," which Peggy Lee later covered, a recording that became the biggest hit of her career. The Famous Flames toured a lot with Little Willie, but that all ended one night in 1964, just after I had recorded and released my latest single, "Out of Sight." On the strength of that hit, we were going back into the Apollo, as headliners this time, when the news came down that Little Willie John had been arrested in Seattle for killing a man. It happened at Little Willie John's engagement party. Some fellow got into a tussle with him over, of all things, seating. The argument got out of hand, they fought, and Little Willie stabbed him to death.

So they put him away and let him rot in jail until the day he died. I had tried for more than a year to get him sprung, and we actually did manage to get him out, but it proved to be a brief taste of freedom, because he was soon arrested again in L.A. for violating his parole. They put him back in jail, and this time for good. I went up to Seattle to see him a few times while he was in the slammer and was shocked to see how this once robust entertainer had become so frail that he was wheelchair bound, hacking and sniffing with pneumonia that he had picked up in his cold prison cell. I vowed I would get him out again, but he just shook his head. He looked into my eyes and said evenly, "The only way I'm ever going to get out is horizontally."

They had broken him by taking away his power and his influence.

Later that year I recorded one of my most personal albums, *Thinking About Little Willie John and a Few Nice Things*.

In my opinion, if Little Willie John had been White, he would have been as influential as Elvis Presley. Don't get me wrong—I loved Elvis. He was a friend of mine, even though I knew that he copied about 75 percent of what he did from me: going with the gospel-type sound in "Heartbreak Hotel," to the hip-swiveling dancing, to the jumpsuits, right down to the cape, which I have to say flattered me so very much.

But I loved Little Willie John just as much, and I always felt that God had chosen to save me from a fate that could have been just as bad as his. Anyone over fifty remembers what it was like in America for a poor Black man with no special talents to try to grow up without getting into some sort of trouble, deserved or otherwise, from certain types who had a special fondness for matching up Black necks with the nearest tree. My daddy saw it all and whenever we were alone he used to tell me to watch out for myself because no matter what, the White man was never going to change, because he couldn't.

I never forgot those words, especially when I heard the news that Little Willie had died, and again when I myself touched bottom in my own life. But as I say, I was fortunate because the Almighty had decided to spare me the worst of the consequences by giving me the special kind of talent that He did. Along with it, He made certain that I had the strength to resist most temptations, and the desire to want to straighten up and stand tall, no matter how hard the many invitations to Hell were for me to resist.

I guess that is why early on, while still struggling to make it in show business, I decided that no one could do better for me, or by me, than me—and that's what gave me the courage and the conviction to take over the reins of my own destiny. After all, who out there knew better than me how to do what I could do? I had created something of myself out of my own head, and I was the only one who really knew what that was. And I was confident enough to put my own money up to prove it.

Returning to play the Apollo in 2003 brought as much life back to the old place as it did in renewing my own professional life. In the end, performing is still my job, and the Apollo is still my main office, and that made my return an act of faith and duty as much as a gesture of love.

It surprised me to see how much the Apollo had changed through the years. Most notably how, in the wake of Harlem's so-called Renaissance, for all intents and purposes the once proud and independent theater was now owned and operated by the government! That reality startled me because in so many ways, so was I. At least financially. I have had to struggle for many years to maintain my dignity, my creative soul, and my way of life, in times of racial strife and financial stress. Like the venerable Apollo, I have had my days of glory and my days of decline.

Throughout my career, I've always wanted to stay at the grass-roots level, where I thought the action was, to be known as the people's man. And it was for that reason that I always preferred playing the old, precorporate Apollo to, say, any downtown Palace or Radio City Music Hall. I always liked playing for the foot soldiers rather than for the generals. I have always cherished my connection to the ghetto, the low-income communities, White or Black, to the people who best connect to my music. I am grateful in my life for never having abandoned the social roots of my creativity. In the end I am still a working-class man, and the only kingdom I belong to is the one that God blesses.

I know that whenever I walk out on to a stage, any stage, nobody wants to pay their good, hard-earned money to see their own misery reflected back at them. That is why, when the spotlight comes on, I am transformed into the happiest man in the world. At that moment, I *am* the happiest man in the world, the happiest man who ever lived, ready, willing, and able to shine my happiness down onto the people.

Of course, it wasn't always that way, especially in the beginning.

TWO

I WAS BORN IN A SHACK IN THE BACKWOODS OF BARNSWELL, South Carolina, and a good part of my genetic makeup is Apache American Indian. I believe I was actually descended from Geronimo. My daddy, whose Christian name was James Joe Brown Jr., had an original Indian name that meant "Gardener," because he was good at working the land. That was the Indian way, to be named after what you did. Later on, like so many other names, it was changed to Brown by the White man, after the color of his skin. That's why there are so many Browns in the South today, Brown being the Black equivalent of the White name Smith, which probably comes from blacksmiths. I also have some Chinese in me, at least as much as I have Black (and maybe a little Egyptian King Tut thrown in for good measure). All you have to do is look at my face—it's all there. And my size. I'm Tut small, but so are all the little guys in the movies I loved—James Cagney for one, Robert Blake for another.

Speaking of Robert Blake, I can relate to him because of all that he's going through now. I followed his career from when he was a kid, in those *Our Gang* comedies he made, and then as the sidekick for Don Barry as Red Ryder in the old movies. One day I ran into him and he introduced himself to me, and told me he was a fan of mine. We talked to each other for a long time. I told him I dug him, and he said he dug me, all the way back to "Please Please Please," and I told him I remembered him as Little Beaver. Man, he jumped out of his shoes and I knew we were down!

Both Cagney and Blake played men with chips on their shoulders put there by other people. I always felt that in their hearts, they were Black men playing White men so that mainstream audiences could understand their suffering. But to me, they were Black.

Cagney played a tough guy who smacked around women in the movies. And audiences loved him for it. Blake was accused of killing his wife, and they want to lynch him. That more than anything else made me love him all the more—not for what he may have done, but for the judgments that were made before he had his day in court. It reminds me of nothing so much as a Black man standing trial in the Old South.

Watching these heroes, these brothers I identified with, showed me that it wasn't going to be easy making it in Whitey Smith's world no matter what color you were. It was a flickering world that as a child was so near to me and yet so far. My daddy, who tried to raise me on his own, also tried to protect me from it for as long as he could. But a day came when he couldn't do it anymore and he reluctantly took me to Augusta's south side to be raised by my aunt Honey with all my other cousins, while Daddy was taken by the Navy. He did well in the service because he was used to taking orders and not questioning White authority. Every so often he'd come back to Augusta to visit me. He'd stay the night and leave early the next morning. If it was difficult for him, it was even more so for me. I couldn't understand why he had just given me away like that, so that he could just come and go. In those days I was too young to understand the difference between love and responsibility. I wanted my daddy all to myself, and when I couldn't have any of him, I felt I had none of him.

I missed my mother as much, if not more, than my daddy. She was only about twenty miles away in South Carolina, but it might as well have been the other side of the universe for all that I saw of her. Which was never.

In the Old South that I grew up in, in the late thirties and early forties, there was no such thing as subsidized child care, or anything close to it. There was a saying in the air back then: "If a mule dies, you buy another; if a Black dies, you hire another." That meant that if you got sick the State didn't care whether you died or recovered. If you passed away, there were one hundred more lined up to take your place. There was so little interest in keeping us alive that when it came to our health, they couldn't have cared less.

Dental care? I had genetically bad gums as a kid, no way to take care of my teeth, and no dentist available to me. As a result I lost all of my teeth at an early age to pyorrhea, made worse by a lack of a proper diet, conditions that are largely avoidable with even the most basic of professional care. Today I have implants, which are a godsend. Back then, once I lost my teeth, it only made my bite all that much meaner.

I have carried the fire and rage that came with the poverty, the family breakdowns, and the social indifference I experienced as a child inside of me all these years, because it was so deeply a part of my growing up. Like so many other poor Southern Black boys and girls, I have never been able to completely shake the curse of fear. My welfare and well-being made no difference to anyone, and there was nothing for me to look forward to in life; by the time I was five, I feared there would never be a way out or up from the endless poverty we were engulfed by.

Aunt Honey lived on the edge of the Black terry. On the other side of the street were all these pretty houses where the White people lived. On our side it was strictly Shantyville. We lived that close to the Whites, but in truth we were worlds apart. Two different communities that might as well have existed on two different planets—that's how deep the divide really was.

My daddy never went past the second grade in school, my mother the fourth. To scratch out a living, Daddy took whatever jobs he could get, like cutting pine trees, which he said put him in touch with the Earth. I always remember him telling me that pine was the number one tree in the world because of the way it cleans and sweetens the air. It's called an evergreen, he said, because it's forever young and always in season. That's the first thing I wanted to be, I thought back then. A Black evergreen.

Like my parents, I didn't get very far in school, because I had to drop out at the age of ten and try to earn some money for Aunt Honey and all my cousins living together in that house. Today I know I received all the education I would ever need directly from God, but at the time I didn't much care about such things as book learning. Maybe I was too dumb, maybe I was too smart. Either way, school just never interested or excited me all that much. The real action came at night, after all the good little boys and girls were put to bed, their bellies full and their heads spinning with fairy tales. That's when I hit the streets, dancing for pennies and shining shoes for nickels, trying to earn enough money to help put some food on our table. Earning money—now *that* excited me. And because I could sometimes make as much as ten dollars a day, I thought I had already learned everything I would ever need to know.

Dancing, in particular, made me feel like I was somebody. Not long after I moved to Aunt Honey's, I felt that somebody needed a new name. And "Junior" was not going to cut it. So one day, I woke up and decided that, since no one was going to give me a new name, I would change it myself. I dropped the Junior that I had carried around like a crutch since birth. My father, also a Junior himself, named me Junior as well, but I wanted something short, easy to remember, with a rhythm that sounded right, with no unnecessary appendages to drag me down. I wanted to sound like one of my heroes. JAMES BROWN!

You see, growing up, like all kids, I had heroes. Mine were the cowboys of the Western movies. There's a cable channel I get down at my house these days that plays nothing but Westerns, and that's the station I watch more than any other. I love the old cowboys, men like Wild Bill Elliott (I told that to Mr. Reagan when I saw him once at the White House, and he roared his approval), Johnny Mack Brown, Tom Mix, Red Ryder, Hopalong Cassidy, the Lone Ranger. They were simple men, all about good and evil, and they always had their faithful companions, like Gabby Hayes—who, bless his heart, had no teeth—or California or Cannonball. I loved those guys because they were always so smart, so sensible, and so *loyal* (especially when they went after the robbers rather than the "redskins").

And of course, they could fight. Even Bob Steele, who was a wiry little guy. I applied the lesson I learned from him to my own life in the street, a lesson that kept me alive. A big guy can't beat a little guy if the little guy knows how to take care of himself. Little guys are faster and more desperate exactly because the other guys are so big. When I was a kid, whenever I fought in the street, I always made sure the other guy didn't get to me before I got to him. And if he was bigger, which they always were—bullies don't like to pick on the big guys—I'd just see it as being an advantage. I had more of a target to hit and I'd get right up in his face and give it to him. I'd put my arms around a guy who thought he was tough, hang on tight, and run into a wall with him. When I'd back up, the guy would go down. That's called survival in the streets.

I saw something recently that struck a chord in me, while I was watching an old Don Barry Western on cable. In his younger days, Don Barry was the hero, and he always had a sidekick. Later on, he *became* the sidekick, and that shocked me. I didn't think that was so great. I took that as a red flag, a reminder about my own life. I made a kind of rule for myself right then and there: it's better to go from the sidekick to the hero, like Robert Blake did when he went from being Little Beaver to Barretta, than to go from the hero to the sidekick, like Don Barry. Once I got to the center spotlight, I never wanted to give it up, and I knew if I ever did, I was being relegated—or worse, relegating myself, like Don Barry—to permanent sidekick status.

I also have another kind of reminder I always keep nearby,

a memento that I found in Africa and paid a good deal of money for, and that to me is just as valuable as any gold record or award I've ever won, and far more fearsome. It is an original set of extraordinarily heavy shackles and chains that were once used on slaves. These chains sat at the bottom of the ocean for three hundred years until they were salvaged from the wreckage of a sunken slave transport. I had them cleaned up and now I keep them as reminder of one of the reasons my journey upward as an individual, and our journey upward as a people, has been so difficult, especially in America. Despite the Civil War and the Emancipation Proclamation, we were never allowed to run free. That doesn't just mean we couldn't escape, or that we couldn't relocate after the war, but that we couldn't make any real social progress. We couldn't compete, not because we didn't have the ability, but because we didn't have the preparation. The lack of education was just as restricting as the weight of these chains that hung around our feet, hands, neck—and soul. Frederick Douglass said something I've always kept close to me. "You can't enslave an educated man." Educate a man, any man, and then you can relax and let him do what he wants to do. You'll never have to give that man anything if you open up the door and let him get it for himself. Don't give him a handout—give him a way out.

It took a long time for me to understand how to take the shackles off of myself. Like so many others, I thought the key to the locks was in the hands of the Man. It took a lifetime to realize that all I had to do was spread my arms to the sky, and the shackles would fall by themselves.

And that's exactly what I did the night of December 7, 2003, when I was honored with a Kennedy Center Award, given to me for the unique and valuable contributions they had deemed I made to the cultural life of our nation. What they were really giving me was the right to drop those chains for the last time.

I spent that week at the White House, and all the while I kept rubbing my wrists, amazed at the feeling of recognized freedom. I never forgot for a minute that my people started in this country in the outhouse. For a second I felt like Moses, the head driver of his people, and I thought, wouldn't it be amazing if I put a stick down in front of the president and it turned into a snake, and then I asked the president to "Let *all* my people go!"

Hey, look now, don't get me wrong. I love this country very much. I consider myself a patriot. I am proud to be an American, and of all that I have accomplished. To me, the order of priorities is clear: God, country, family. I consider the Kennedy Center Award a great honor—I thank God for it, and I see it as a sign that I really did have a fair measure of influence on some people after all: not just Black people or White people, but *all* people, and not just in the States but throughout the world. The award is an acknowledgment of my place, despite all the nastiness and lies and exaggerations that have been written about me through the years. In a very real sense, the music spoke quite elegantly for me, as to who I am, who I wanted to be, and what I wanted to do with my life. The award is a symbol to me of freedom, that whenever I get onstage, the satisfaction I still get from performing the way I want to is met and felt by those in the audience who have come to see me. It is a way of proving to myself over and over that free people come to see me, to hear what I have to say, and to enjoy the way I say it. That is a precious exchange, perhaps the most profound in the world. Being on the stage is, for me, everything from a physical liberation to a type of religious redemption.

I thank the Kennedy Center so much for giving me their honor, and allowing me to retain my own. Nevertheless, for a long time prior to my receiving the award, and for a little while after, whenever I have made some especially great leap, and the tabloid press and gossipmongers kick in with their dirt, I can't help but feel that while making a name for myself as a Black man in America in a field where creativity and sexuality are factors, one hand wins awards for me and the other is an invitation to those in power to put those shackles right back on me, tighter than ever.

THREE

I THINK YOU'RE STARTING TO GET THE PICTURE. To understand where my music comes from is to understand
where I come from, and in order to do that, it's necessary to look at the culture that produced me, and the single most relevant issue of that culture—race. Let's stop
here for a second to look at the big picture of race in
America today, as I see it. Take the carmaker Ford, only as
an example. Taurus is a Ford. Thunderbird is a Ford. Scor-
pio is a Ford. They're all different, yet they're all Ford auto-
mobiles. America's multiculturism is like Ford, only
instead of cars we comprise all types of races—African,
Asian, European, Latin—with a multicultural history that
is not always recognized and acknowledged for what it has
to offer. We need everybody to fill out the big picture.

Everyone has something special to contribute to this country. Take the Chinese, for example. Not only were they instrumental in building America's infrastructure, but they are extraordinary with food, among the best chefs in the country, if not the world. Yet in America, most of them are still relegated to the Chinatowns, or cheap roadside stops, or malls. This downgrading of our cultural resources remains one of our greatest problems. America is not just a country of wealthy White folks anymore. It should be a place where any young person, man or woman, Black, White, Asian, Latin, should have the right and, perhaps even more important, the *belief* in the right to do whatever he or she wants with his or her life. The word *can't* should not exist in the hopes and dreams of any young American today.

Now musicians have always had the right idea about all of this. If those in power back in the late forties and fifties held the lock on the future of America, R & B, soul, country, and rock and roll were the keys that set the next generation free. The music was not just *about* rebellion—*it was the rebellion itself*. Before rock and roll, no generation rebelled as a unit, at least not through music. Instead, they *reflected*, using what had come before as their yardstick for the future. Then came the new music, and suddenly they, we, *I* had something all my own to contribute. *And it was good, man!* My music and the music of my generation changed all of our lives because it changed our values, our desires, and ultimately our accomplishments. I sure as hell wouldn't be writing any of this down, and you sure as hell wouldn't be reading even a word of it, if it wasn't for the music. Elvis, Bill Haley, Little Richard, Fats Domino, Jerry Lee Lewis, Chuck Berry—all those first-generation pioneers brought something to young people nobody had ever heard before. These cats were all into something new that wasn't already redolent in the air.

Speaking of my good friend Little Richard, whom I love dearly, he still insists he was the one who discovered me, and you know what? It's true! It sounds crazy but that's the way it happened.

He was living in Macon, but came to Toccoa, Georgia, where I was playing with the Famous Flames. We had been making some noise all over the state, and he wanted to find out why. He caught our show, and afterward, he went and told his manager back in Macon, Mr. Clint Bramley (Bramley later became my manager as well for a brief period).

"Mr. Clint," he said, "I've just seen the best group I've ever seen in my life, and the fellow fronting it is James Brown. James Brown and His Famous Flames." Not long after, I went to Macon, and then, with Mr. Bramley, to California for the first time.

The only problem for me was that Little Richard, as far as I was concerned, was strictly rock and roll. He was a pi-ano pounder, seemingly chained to the instrument, while I was chained to nothing. He geared his show to mostly White audiences, and that was fine. I, on the other hand, was much more raw and stayed strictly within the confines of what I knew: soul. I had no interest then—and never have since—in being a rock-and-roll musician. I like rock and roll—don't misunderstand me—but I didn't want to convert any soul performers, including myself, to rock and roll; nor was I interested in converting any rock and rollers to soul, Little Richard included. They were doing their thing, and I was doing mine.

Elvis, of course, is another story. In addition to all his music, he brought rebellion into teen fashion. For me, the look I had—the suits, the cape—was something else, something more personal. Elvis wore those tight pants, and at the time, I wore tight pants, too, and when I saw him up there on the stage for the first time dressed that way, I said to myself, Hey, that's *me up there*! And that was all right! Elvis was the one who made it okay not just to show some of your body, but to show some of it *off*, and once he did, no one, not the newspapers, not the record industry, not Ed Sullivan, could stop him, although they all tried. I may have been first, but he was White, and that made him untouchable. And maybe even more important, how much of a leap was it then, really, from Elvis liberating the music of a generation of uptight White kids to a few years later when those same kids—now a little older—gathered the courage to march in the streets of the South for civil rights?

I knew Elvis personally, almost from the beginning of both our careers. He was a lot different from what most people believed. Offstage he was very quiet, very polite, and never arrogant or pushy. In that respect, he was one of the most pleasant people ever to be around. Whenever he'd see me, or when we met up in some club, we'd always ask each other how we were, and sooner or later the subject would revert to his favorite topic—gospel music. He knew that I had come out of that sound, and he would ask me a million questions about it: where it came from, how I sang it, what I felt when I did it, how the music related to my life, my arrangements, all of it. He could never get enough of that, and I was happy to give it to him.

Of course, he took a lot of my style and my teachings and put them into his own music, something that I didn't mind at all. The idea in my head was to spread the glory of gospel, and if rock and roll could do that, especially among White folks, well, that was just fine.

One time I was doing a gig on Sunset Boulevard, along the notorious strip, at a club that doesn't exist anymore. A lot has changed since then, but during its day, the Sunset Strip was the center of the rock-and-roll universe. The place was called the Trip, located not very far from today's House of Blues, and sure enough, I was there for only a few minutes when I bumped right into Elvis. The bill included Gerry and the Pacemakers, Tommy Sands (who had married Nancy Sinatra and become Frank Sinatra's son-in-law for a brief period of time), the Temptations, and Billy J. Kramer. It was one of those shows where everybody did a song or two and the next act came on. I was sitting backstage when all of a sudden Elvis appeared. Now he was not the sort of fellow who barhopped or hung out with a crowd. It was highly unusual for him to be seen in public that way, but apparently he had heard I was going to be there, and he had wanted to see me before I went on. He knocked on my door, and when I opened it and saw Elvis standing there, we hugged, and I invited him into my dressing room. "Elvis," I said, "what can I do for you?"

"Well," he said, "I'd like to sing a little gospel with you if you don't mind."

I didn't, not at all, and for the next twenty minutes or so we did a couple of tunes. I could tell he had been practicing, and I guess he wanted to test himself out. After that, he thanked me, we hugged again, and he disappeared out my door. No one else saw him that night, and I don't believe he stayed for the show. That was Elvis—when it came to his image and his music, he could be shadowy and intense, in that order.

Elvis Presley wanted everything James Brown had because, in addition to gospel, he wanted to somehow get into soul. I had a man working for us by the name of Bob Patton, and Elvis used to call him all the time to get my tapes so that he could play them until he thought he had the sound down. Then he'd rent a theater for himself and just some friends so he could perform soul music, James Brown–style.

Not long after he asked me if he could use my band as a backup for a tour, but I couldn't go for that. This was my band, and my band only. Still, I loved the boy.

Marlon Brando was another early rock-and-roll hero of mine, although he never sang a rock, R & B, or soul song in his life. Nevertheless, he was a cultural icon for rebellion. In 1954, he made a movie that shook the youth of America down to its motorcycle boots. It was called *The Wild One*. The way he looked, the way he dressed all in black leather, the attitude, the youth, and the cultural scream he produced—all of it put him right up there with the Elvises and the Robert Johnsons of the world—forerunners to the seismic shift that American youth was about to effect.

In the movie, a pretty young White girl says to Brando's character, "Johnny, what are you rebelling against?" To which he replies with a sneer, "Whattaya got?" That moment of two-stroke fury and frustration fuel-injected a generation with high-octane angst. Everyone who came after Brando used a style he had created. He may never have sung a note, but he was rock and roll to his cut-time core. A generation later, the afterburn of Brando's image was strong enough to inspire the youth movement toward racial integration that was hung on the hopes and dreams of his generation.

Elvis and Brando were both what I call a man's man. They did what they did, they sang songs, they playacted and were never girlish about any of it. Far from it! The ladies idolized them because they were pretty, but the guys admired their strength and manliness and looked to them for *direction*. Years later, their same kind of bravado was carried on in the movies by Sylvester Stallone, Charles Bronson, Peter Falk, and Robert Blake, all of whom were down with focusing the eyes and the ears of their fans toward something that went beyond the messages in their individual films.

And I did it, too. What's more, I can tell you the exact moment when I went from being a soul singer to a cultural icon. It happened with the "One."

Getting down with the "One" is the whole key to understanding my music, where it came from and where it went. I don't call it the Two because the "One" stands alone at the head of the beat, with force, leadership, and most important, self-pride. I don't know what the actual musical origins for the "One" are because I never heard it in Beethoven or Tchaikovsky or even Gershwin, or in any of the earlier songs I myself had written. But I do know this: Black musicians, historically, if instinctively, even if we didn't know what to call it, never hesitated to hit it on the "One." We were actually playing a variation of it all along and simply didn't know it, going back to early blues and gospel. The "One" was an extension of our life experiences, when we always began our music on the downbeat.

One day I might have been fooling around with the guitar and hit a riff I liked, or maybe I was noodling on the piano and suddenly discovered something that was there already in my head. I don't read music, so most of the time when I'm writing, the way I start off a new song is to find out how to make the melody work on the instrument I'm using at the moment. It really doesn't matter what I play it on, because God has already given me the master sheet. After He's done that, it's up to me to put it onto the James Brown music assembly line. I'm just the messenger, then, in this process, not the originator.

The "One" is derived from the Earth itself, the soil, the pine trees of my youth. And most important, it's on the upbeat—ONE two THREE four, not the downbeat, one TWO three FOUR—that most blues are written in. Hey, I know what I'm talking about! I was *born* to the downbeat, and I can tell you without question there is no pride in it. The upbeat is rich. The downbeat is poor. Stepping up proud only happens on the aggressive "One," not the passive Two, and never on lowdownbeat. In the end, it's not about music—it's about life.

The "One" was not just a new kind of beat; it was a statement of race, of force, of stature, of stride. It was the aural equivalent of standing tall and saying *Here I am*, of marching with strength rather than tiptoeing with timidity.

It was something that once I delivered it, everyone tried to copy, and I don't blame them. Everyone wants to copy from the best. The only thing I don't like is how today they have programmed machines to try to copy the human sound of the "One." Machines can't do what I did—they haven't got a chance. Why? Because there has to be an element of the human imperfection to the beat, of the chance emphasis, of the identification with the cultural origins of the beat. Otherwise, no matter how well programmed, or maybe because of it, the music always sounds to me like canned food. And that's okay. Plenty of people have to exist on that stuff when there's no real food around. But if there's only canned food in the world, people will quickly forget what the taste of the real thing is, and the canned food will replace the original and become the new standard measure. That, my friends, is not good. So you see, that is why the "One" is more than a new beat. The "One" is a way of life expressed through the music of James Brown.

Once I have the basic sound, then I work on it with the band members to try to come up with an arrangement that fits the mood and meaning of the song. And then, when it's ready, the "One" gets fits onto it, like a custom saddle, until it is the proper equivalent to the way I strut onto a stage at the start of my show, with my head held high, my feet taking wide strides, and a big smile on my face. Then I hear the audience cheering, and I know all over again that no matter what may be going on in my life, I am living on the "One." And because of it, for the next two hours everything is going to be all right.

"I Feel Good" is one of my early songs that contained conscious elements of the "One." I cut a version of that song in Chicago, but didn't release it because something was missing for me. The intro was a light keyboard thing that kind of danced over the melody, then went into this jumpy, staccato, sharp 1-2-3-4 beat that I thought at the time was a little *too* sharp. *Deedle deedle deedle dee.* That didn't do it for me.

The next time I tried to record the song a couple of years later, I was in Jacksonville, Florida. I remember one day I woke up and heard the sound of the opening clearly in my head. It still had the *deedle deedle deedle dee*, but now I heard the bottom—*dum dum da dum.* Yes! I knew I had to contact Mr. Bobbit, my manager, right away.

While I was still with Mr. Nathan's label, I had replaced Mr. Nathan as my manager with Charles Bobbit. He was somebody I knew and trusted, and eventually came to love. Mr. Bobbit and I have been through a lifetime of adventures together—he has been my moral support and my creative sounding board. I know him, I love him, and I trust him. No more so than when I dialed his number that day.

I reached Mr. Bobbit in his room and told him to drop everything because we had to immediately leave for Miami. "For what?" he said with bleary eyes and a scratchy voice.

"I have to go to Criterion Studios and recut 'I Feel Good.'"

Twenty minutes later we were in a plane heading for Miami.

As we worked, I began to shift the rhythm, moving the second part—that *dum dum da dum*—*over* the first part, and I did it to a one-three rhythm: *DUM dum DA dum*. That was it! That was the sound I was looking for! The song now had the masculine heft of the bass that it needed. Even though it wasn't completed in the "One," it anticipated what was coming—a solid, important, even crucial step forward in the evolution of what would come to be known as the James Brown sound.

I keep my band together as a well-disciplined group, and when we're recording we become kind of an ROTC unit. That is to say, when they're rehearsing, I always want my band to be in uniform, in their stage clothes. Some of them will tell you that because of my disciplinary demands James Brown is a difficult man to work for. Am I? You better believe I am! Entertainment, feeling good onstage, doing your thing is difficult if you do it right. Any major director in the movies and any winning coach in sports is going to be hard to work for. Difficulty is not the thing that matters. What does is the ability to make a film work, or make a team win. Or a record sing. Anyone who works for me has got to work hard, or else they aren't strong enough to be a part of the James Brown Revue. I've never been afraid of hard work. In fact, I'm proud of it. I've been called the Hardest-Working Man in Show Business. I like that name because it signifies a connection to my blue-collar roots and defines the intensity of the work that goes into making my music.

To me, putting on a show means exactly that—putting on a *show*. It's all a part of the performance, and the performance depends upon the music. That means it all begins with the writing of a song. If you aren't seeing the spectacle that is the fruit of my labors when I'm onstage, then you've been duped. You're seeing someone else who's calling himself James Brown—it's as simple as that. I've been around forever, and I've seen all the changes that have taken place in the music business. I'm one of the very last acts that actually works his band in rehearsal until I'm confident they understand that they are not just playing some notes together, but putting on a spectacle: a James Brown performance!

The roots of this approach are derived from three places. I've always loved those film clips from the forties of the immortal Louis Jordan. His band had a great style, and he always gave a complete presentation, right down to that beautiful girl sitting on the piano with her legs crossed and her dress raised just a little above her knees. That always knocked me out, and still does!

The second place is comic books. I loved comic books when I was a kid. I used to read them whenever I could get my hands on one, and the visuals left me in awe. Anything could happen, and everything did, within the confines of those panels. To me those panels were like the outline of a stage, or the screen of a movie theater, where there was always a great show being put on. If you see my Revue from the back of the theater, with all the color, animation, lighting, and costumes, you'll discover one of my secrets—I'm like the comics: the element of great art and color surrounds, enhances, and electrifies the entire presentation.

The third element was the image of Gorgeous George, the wrestler who became one of the great early stars of live TV. He took something that, again, I had first seen in the comic books—Superman's cape—and adapted it for his own stylistic use. I remember I began using a towel one extra-warm night in Chattanooga during a show, when the spirit suddenly hit me, like something straight out of all the gospel revival meetings I had attended. Suddenly I was like a preacher in a church. After I saw Gorgeous George on TV, and realized he had added a special flamboyance to his matches, I began to use the towel for more than the practical need to wipe off my sweat. It became a prop, just like preachers use handkerchiefs in Southern churches. The towel eventually became a cape, which I used for maximum dramatic effect, and then, when Elvis saw me, and saw the same effect that I did when I first witnessed Gorgeous George, he made it a part of his show as well.

All these elements helped to create the James Brown you see onstage. Everything I did was geared toward a single goal: to be accepted by the audience for who I am and what I do. That's the real reason why I eventually had to leave the Flames and start a solo career. I realized early on that I didn't want to be part of any crowd, buried in the anonymity of a group, because I had something special and different of my own, something I needed to get out there. Part of it was the way I looked and sounded, with my high pompadour, my tight clothes, the cape, the scream, the groan in my voice, the splits, and the creation and adaptation of the "One." All of these things went into the realization of the James Brown I wanted the world not just to know, but to love.

In 1965 the release of "Papa's Got a Brand New Bag" changed everything again for me and for my music, from the lyrics to the high-energy beat to the very nature of what soul music was and all that it could be. As Dick Clark might say, now you could *dance* to it!

Still, it nearly gave Mr. Syd Nathan of my label then,

King Records, a heart attack! He simply didn't want to put it out. He couldn't see how it could be a hit, and kept asking me what this crazy song was all about. I looked at him, smiled, shrugged my shoulders, and told him I had no idea either! All I knew for sure, I said, was that it had to have come from someplace so deep inside of me and that it had to have been put there by a higher power.

Mr. Nathan shrugged his shoulders, shook his head, and never mentioned it again.

1965 was rife with fresh sounds, coming from a world of Black music merging onto the mainstream (and White) pop charts. Otis Redding, Aretha Franklin, all the Motown singers, Ray Charles, all of them side by side with the Beatles, the Rolling Stones, Bob Dylan, the Righteous Brothers and Dean Martin. They were recording what would one day come to be known as the great American music of their day. For me, the rest of it was old news. One of my favorite songs of the fifties had been "Oh My Papa," sung with the accent on the second "pa," the way they pronounced it in old White Europe. It was a huge hit for that wonderful singer Eddie Fisher, who carried the sound of old Europe in an inflection that his generation had grown up with (and Eddie even did it in waltz time!).

When I wrote "Papa's Got a Brand New Bag," I made sure that the first word in the song, *Papa*, had an American-style emphasis. From the opening beat there came a necessary shift in the rhythm of the words, with the "One" emerging in the way *Papa* was pronounced. That set the tone and the melody and the beat of the song: *Papa's Got a Brand New Bag.*

I had discovered the power of the percussive upbeat, using the rhythm in an untraditional way, rather than with the horns, or the pianos, or the guitars or the stand-up bass, the standard instruments of R & B. I didn't use them to open the song because I didn't need them anymore! I didn't need "melody" to make music. That was, to me, old-fashioned and out of step. I now realized that I could compose and sing a song that used one chord or at the most two. Although "Papa's Got A Brand New Bag" has just two chords, and a melody sung over what is really a single note, it is just as musical as anything Pavarotti has ever sung. More important, it stood for everything I was about—pride, leadership, strength, intensity. And it went straight to number one on every pop and R & B chart in the world.

Nevertheless, I can so clearly remember how no one— *no one*—got it when I first introduced the song to the band. The drummers couldn't move their sticks in their hands to the ONE *two* THREE *four* progression I asked for as a replacement to the *one* TWO *three* FOUR they had always played or, more precisely, the *one* AND *two* AND *three* AND *four* AND—the basic rhythm of rock and roll that stretched all the way back to Chuck Berry.

To me, the song represented so many things at once—

the sound of my people, the beat underneath their social contribution, the rise of Black music into the mainstream, the continuing struggles and victories of the civil rights movement, and just about every aspect of the culture that was happening at the time. And all that had come before. The song, done in the "One," represented a collective summation of how the culture and the music of the sixties had combined to take a giant leap forward—for James Brown as a person and an artist, and for Black music entering into the conscience (and the record collection) of mainstream America.

It was like opening the floodgates to a rhythm-based extension of soul, a physically performed, roots-derived configuration of music that comes straight from the heart. In that sense, soul became the perfect marching music for the civil rights era, a way to choreograph the burgeoning pride that could be found everywhere. It was, to me, like the jump beat that we always saw in films from Africa, when the Blacks were organizing against apartheid. We'd always see them jumping in place, with the sound of the drum beneath them, giving them weight, lending them focus, providing them unity.

What was missing for me and my people was the rhythm of our own revolution—a soundtrack strong enough to bring us to the outside rather than to keep us on the inside.

What had always bothered me most about the early

days of the civil rights movement was that there was still no organized, external way for Black people to get together and express their anger and frustration as a unit after four centuries of being the White man's punching bag. Saying "stop hitting me" was the most difficult thing to get Black people to do, especially in the South, where I came from. That was one of the things I most wanted to do through my music—to teach Black people how to very nicely say, "I'm sorry but you're not going to do that to me anymore. I'm too strong, I'm too young, I'm too tough, and most of all, I'm too proud."

Pride—that was the key. Pride and self-worth. I was never into an eye for an eye, a tooth for a tooth—to me, that was war council talk and it belonged to the more militant factions of the civil rights movement. I was more for winning a slice of that very sweet American pie called success for my people. I wanted us to be brought in, not shut out. And I figured I could do that as I always did: with my music.

All that was left was for me to find a way to say *funk it!*

In the mid-sixties, funk was still struggling to be born. While recording "Papa's Got a Brand New Bag," I could feel something new kicking around inside me. Soon enough, I gave birth to a little baby I named funk, a gift delivered by Papa that was to become *everybody's* brand-new bag! I had created something new and important for both Black and White audiences, and like the great Mr. Sinatra, I'm not ashamed to say I did it my way!

People often ask me the difference between soul and funk, and then only if they can get past the fact that, once and forever, what I do is *not* rock and roll! Rock and roll happens to be some of the music that I love, but let's face it: it is a derivative of Black R & B, with some Hank Williams–type country thrown in and maybe a little Midwestern folk, like the music of Woody Guthrie. Roy Brown, for instance, who had a great R & B band, produced the sound that was more or less copied by Bill Haley and the Comets, but it's Bill Haley who gets all the credit for introducing "rockabilly."

The fifties was the era when White people, God bless 'em, tried more than ever to play the blues like the Black performers did, without ever having the faintest notion of where that type of music came from, or why, or how, and of course, by who. Most of them played it on the upbeat, which Alan Freed, the first great radio disc jockey for teens, then called rock and roll. Now every Black man who ever lived knows that traditional blues starts on the downbeat. Because of that simple rhythmic mistake, a lot of the times White folks attempted to play blues it sounded just plain corny, because they couldn't capture the essential rhythm of it. They couldn't read it right. And so how, of course, could they possibly play it? No matter *what* terry they grew up in!

I'm not saying this is true for *every* White performer. Some of them learned through the years what the blues were actually all about. Eric Clapton, for instance. B. B. King likes Mr. Clapton, too. He says he's all right and that's good enough for me. But Mr. Clapton *learned* how to play the blues. He wasn't born with the music in him, even if he has become one of the best bluesmen out there. My hat is off to him as a master, and my hat is off to him as a student.

But as far as what I do, certainly there's some rhythm and blues in my music. I may even do a couple of rock-type songs, some jazz, and there are always romantic ballads to be sung every night of the week. But no matter what, everything I do begins with *feeling*. Soul music comes directly from the heart—it's let-it-all-hang-out music that has a deep, direct connection to the soul. I could sing *Pagliacci*, or "It Had to be You," or "It's a Man's Man's Man's World," or "Please Please Please," or any type of gospel tune, and because I'm working off of a feeling, I'm essentially singing to and for myself. It doesn't matter if anyone else is listening or not. It's for me, about me, about the environment I came out of.

Look at, say, Mike Tyson, the kind of fighter he is, and you can clearly see the environment he grew up in right on his face. I believe that if he had been raised in the South he would have been an entirely different fighter, and his career would have gone in a completely different direction. The White North made him too angry, too mean, and no one was capable enough of helping him focus his abilities in a positive way. That is something you can't impersonate or approximate.

It's the same deal with my music. What I sing is either real, lived, taken in, and then given back, or it's not the kind of music that I have any connection to. That's why it is inconceivable for James Brown to have been born and raised, say, in Massachusetts, and be the soul and funk performer that he is. My environment—the slums of the South—*created* me, and I in turn created the music that that environment connected me to. It's all a giant circle of life, endless and continuous as the shape of an old vinyl record or a new CD.

I think the rich cultural heritage that came out of ghetto life is one of the reasons Black people never tried to break up the areas they lived in down south. It is my belief that despite the poverty and the racism and all the struggles, the sense of feeling, solidarity, and brotherhood that arises in the ghetto produces a wealth of talent. It is the environment that has kept our people together, in their own neighborhoods and in the neighborhoods created electronically by the network of our music. It has kept us from being forcibly dissipated, and that in turn has allowed us to maintain the originality and energy that makes us who and what we are.

Don't misunderstand me. I'm not saying that segregation

is a good thing. About the only people who ever benefited from segregation were White manufacturers—those clever dudes who realized that segregation meant they could sell two water fountains where only one was needed. No wonder segregation was so hard to conquer! But I'm talking about something entirely different. I'm talking about keeping the unit of the family and the culture of a people intact, and getting the most out of the least, which was the Black experience in America for most of the twentieth century. And I believe this experience directly accounts for the wealth of extraordinary, heartfelt music we produced.

Think of it, if you can, without being distracted by the imagery, as a herd of horses. You want to buy a horse out of a pack. You need the pack to see the individual differences, and make the comparisons. That's when you learn that while they may all look the same from the outside, if you look real closely, you can see how one Appaloosa might run a little faster or has the makings of a Thoroughbred leading the pack. It is the pride among the herd itself that makes the finest horses do their best, not the wranglers who keep them together.

And that, my friends, is where I found myself in the mid-sixties, at the top of the soul game. However, that little baby was starting to open its mouth for attention. And attention is exactly what I gave it. "Funk," I said, "what are you trying to say?" And then it was my turn to listen.

If soul music was all about the heart, than funk was the choreography of those feelings, the manifestation of something real and clean, mixed and measured with a certain Black pride. It became the more showy form of soul, and because of it the audience necessarily got more involved. I don't mean just musically. You can't tell yourself how to funk onstage; it is your musical child that takes you and the rest of the audience to another place through the delivery of a song and a dance, combining the joy that they produce together. For all these reasons, among the many tunes that I recorded in that period, I would have to choose "Say it Loud," which I recorded in February 1968, as one of the most perfect funk performances I ever put out.

I don't think it's any coincidence that funk and the civil rights movement found their voices about the same time. The more embedded we became in the movement, the more self-pride our music expressed. Our music became a ritualistic measure of that pride, while the lyrics became more focused on the day, more politically oriented, but never losing any of its romantic aspects. "Say It Loud, I'm Black and I'm Proud" (written, of course, on the "One") put together all the best elements of Black popular music at the time: Black pride, a reaching out to our White brothers and sisters, and a fair measure of showmanship to prettily wrap the whole thing up—a very nice package, indeed!

Funk has become such a large part of my show today that if I'm into a soul thing and I sense the audience getting restless, I can kick right into "It's a Man's Man's Man's World," and if the audience still isn't responding I can go to "Say It Loud," and let the funk come in to save the day. My one goal is never to lose the audience, never to let them drift or shift their focus, even for a minute, because if that happens that essential connection from my soul to theirs gets weakened, if it doesn't completely break. When I'm onstage, it is the soul of the music that drives the show, that leads the band, that takes control of the audience and me as well and makes everyone smile.

But it's the funk that keeps all of us alive and kicking and screaming for more!

FOUR

MUSIC WASN'T THE ONLY CHANGE IN MY LIFE, OR THE only thing changing my life. I was developing a sound, a style, and a look. What was missing was human reflection. I got some from the audience. What I needed was a more personal connection to myself.

In 1953, at the age of twenty, I got married for the first time. Velma Warren was a wonderful, churchgoing, tall, beautiful God-fearing woman I had met through my affiliation with the Mount Zion Baptist Church. The group I was singing with at the time, Bobby Byrd's Ever Ready Gospel Singers, performed there regularly. One day I was introduced to her and soon enough we became friendly. I started taking her along with us to our local gigs, which turned out to be a very good move, as the other cats who came to see us knew that I wasn't interested in getting tight with any of their women. That was always a problem for me. Wherever I performed, there seemed no shortage of women who wanted to get tight, and I knew wherever there was a gal like that around, there was going to be an angry guy not very far away. Having Velma along saved me from a whole lot of unwanted trouble!

On June 19, 1953, Velma and I were married, in Toccoa, Georgia's, Trinity Church, just about a year after my release from juvenile detention. I was still playing baseball at the time, hoping to make the majors, and I guess I was pretty good because I pitched a no-hitter for the Toccoa team.

However, if things were going all right for me on the ball field and on the stage, my other team—the group I was singing with, the Ever Readys—was starting to come apart at the seams. Mostly out of jealousy. By now I was the undisputed lead singer, and because of it all the songs and arrangements we did were geared to me, and that made the others in the group more than a little upset. Mr. Byrd and I and another member of the band, Sylvester Keels, who realized what the situation was and where the band's future lay, tried to reason with the others. Mr. Byrd reminded them over and over that what was good for one of us was good for all of us. Still, because of the egotistical nature of show business, it was hard to get them to believe we were all working toward the same goal.

That's when someone suggested maybe we should change the name of the group to something a little more dynamic, something with a little heat attached to it. Somebody said, "Hey, what about the Torches?" The Torches was another local band whose main distinction was that they had a White singer in their group. Then somebody else, I don't remember exactly who, shouted out: the Flames. As soon as I heard it I knew. That was it. From that moment on, we were *The Flames*!

So at least we could all agree on one thing: a new name for our group. For the moment, everyone seemed happy, no one more than me. I was playing good ball. I was singing lead in a band I really liked. I had a new bride and a promising future as an athlete and maybe even as an entertainer as well. I was so happy with Velma I began to talk about how maybe we should start our own family so I could correct a few of those cosmic wrongs that had been dealt my way and become the kind of husband to Velma and the kind of father to my own children I never saw or had when I was a boy. I didn't just want to be a daddy—I wanted to be a strong one, to be there for my kids, no matter what the personal sacrifice might be.

Velma agreed with and was excited by my plan and during the next few years we had three sons together, one right after the other.

At first it was like a dream come true. I was happy being a daddy, and doing all the things with my kids that my daddy had never done with me. I began to discover for the first time the secret joy of fatherhood, which not only had eluded me my entire life, but which I had no idea could possibly exist. The sound of one of my boys yelling Daddy was more beautiful to me than any song I had ever written.

Unfortunately, all too soon the strains and conflicts of my professional life began to clash with the idyllic world of Husband and Daddy; and my wife paid the price for that. The first thing that went wrong was I was injured on the ball field. I hurt my knee and my back, seriously enough that I knew that I would never be able to make the pros. After that, I threw all my energies into making it as a singer, and pushed the band and Mr. Byrd harder than I ever had before. The loss of options translated into an intensity of ambition. The only way I knew we could get any kind of real exposure to build a following was to go out and live on the road, 24–7, sometimes for months at a clip, and always without our wives, girlfriends, or kids to get in the way, to distract us from our single goal. We were like a guerrilla army invading the enemy turf of fame. Obviously, it was not a good way to keep a marriage intact. But those were the rules of show business, which became for us the rules of life.

The Flames and I traveled all over the South, doing one-nighters, and what can I say? Yes, there were always girls around, and they seemed to especially like me a whole lot. When you're on the road as much as we were, they become, in an odd way that is difficult for anybody but musicians to fully understand, more of a family to you than your real one. Then the day comes when you realize that the life you're living right now *is the life you're living,* and the one you left at home is the dream. I'm not defending anything I did while I was on the road, and I'm not denying it, either. I'm not saying it was right or wrong—it's just the way of life on the entertainment highway.

Let's say you are a normal workingman. You come home at night, your woman is there, you turn on the radio hoping to catch your favorite song. That one doesn't come on, but others do that you also like a lot. And so you listen to those for a while. Sometimes they become more of a favorite than the one you were waiting to hear. In show business, it's precisely the opposite. You have exactly the music you want because you're making it. If you want to relax with the woman you love, and she's not there, there are other tunes around that, for the moment at least, you can replace her in your emotional Top Ten.

I have been on this planet for a lot of years, and still can't understand how, doing what I do and living how I live, it is possible to make a marriage work. By necessity, love must become the *second* most important thing in a working musician's life if he has any dreams of making it big. I think that's true—that it comes down to the order of priorities in any creative artist's life.

Of course, women may go on their way, too, in marriage

and in their private lives, which is something a lot of men in any field don't realize or take into consideration, or aren't even willing to admit to themselves. Most men want to be the leader of their family, or at least think that's what they want. Which is fine, except they usually marry another leader. Nothing can work when everyone's the boss and no one wants to be second in command. I'm an old-fashioned traditionalist that way, and I readily admit it; when I'm home I like to be the head of my household, and I like to treat women like *women*, not like wives. I love to run around to the other side of a car to open her door, to help her into her coat. I always stand up when they do—I love doing things like that.

By extension, when I go out on the road, I need to know that my woman understands that I'm going to work, as certainly as if I am carrying a lunch bucket under my arm. The women who are a part of the work, no matter how tempting, have very little to do with the woman waiting at home. It's all part of the agreed role of the leader. If it's not clearly defined from day one, it will sooner or later get out of control and introduce a lot of resentment and jealousy to the sanctity of the home. Once that happens, there's no way to stop it.

Instead, it sinks your marriage.

To prevent that, men must strive to remember that marriage is not about instant gratification, or necessarily being with the best-looking woman in the room. Looks really don't matter as much as we think they do when we're young and "in love." Women, we quickly learn, are not perfect objects of fantasy but real-life human beings, just like men, with all the frailties shared. Therefore you've got to know how to compromise and to be able to change, grow, and learn together as a couple in every way—socially, culturally, and economically, hopefully into middle age and beyond. If either wants the other one to stay the way they were on the day they were married, it just won't work. Believe me, I know—I've been there. The ability to stay together, especially in the world of show business, is priceless. When you're lucky enough to find someone you think you can make it with, it's worth fighting to keep her no matter how flexible the rules must, by necessity, be. In other words, you may be able to bend the rules that the two of you have agreed upon, but you can never break them. It is the temper, rather than the tantrum, that keeps you together.

When you make it big, as I did, there's always going to be a part of you that *permanently* belongs to the rest of the world, and your wife must accept that and give up a part of you forever. There's no choice involved in this, and again no right or wrong. It's just the way it is.

I know some of the things I did on the road weren't fair to Velma and the kids, but I didn't think I had any choice if I was going to make a real run at a career in show business. I had chosen a way of life as much as it had chosen me. My music, my band, the road, my fans, and the feeling I got on that stage became so much an essential part of my existence that they became the hands on my life clock. I told time by the next call to go onstage. I saw my future on the road maps that led from one club to the next. Whenever I had any doubts, all I had to do was look out the window of the bus and see bare-chested Black men picking in the cotton fields. That's when I would swear to myself all over again, reaffirm my vows that I was never, ever going to go back to that life, *no matter what*, because if I did, I would be no good to anyone—my wife, my kids, or most important, to myself.

So that was the deal, the bargain I made with my soul. I had no choice and I was smart enough not to kid myself that I did. I still made sure that Velma and the kids had everything they wanted while I continued to live my life the way I had to: high-pomped, decked-out, emotionally double-barreled, and aiming my sights toward the farthest star in the galaxy, without anything even remotely resembling apologies or regrets. To me, that's what losers wallowed in, and I was in this thing to win.

My marriage wasn't the only thing that was coming apart. At the same time, things were continuing to deteriorate between the Flames and me. We had had this string of hits, beginning with "Please Please Please," then "I

Don't Know," "I Feel That Old Feeling Coming On," "No No No," "Why Do You Do Me," "Hold My Baby's Hand," "Chonnie-on-Chon," "Just Won't Do Right," "Let's Make It," and "I Won't Plead No More," among at least a dozen more. Each of them enjoyed some success, particularly "Just Won't Do Right," and we planned our tour around each city with a breakout radio station, arriving in town to coincide with the airplay the song was getting, and doing sellout live shows all over the Eastern seaboard.

On the way we ran into a lot of other great acts. I remember one time we played the famous Palms near Miami, which was one of the top Chitlin Circuit stops on the Southern swing. The bill included such R & B luminaries as the Five Royales, the great Guitar Slim, and Shirley and Lee, who were riding high with "Let the Good Times Roll." Headlining for us were two living legends: B. B. King and the great Ray Charles. Things started out rocky between Ray and me, maybe because we were both such intense performers and he followed me as the closer, never an easy thing for anyone to do. Each of us instinctively knew that nobody could follow us. We were the show-stoppers and show enders. Ray didn't like the fact that I was so young and so strong. And I didn't appreciate having to do battle for top turf. Also, both of us liked a lot of women, and sometimes the same ones. It wasn't until we sat down and talked man-to-man that I could get past my own insecurities and Ray could see for the first time who I really was.

As we got to know each other better, I soon came under his glorious spell, and we became the best of friends. Ray Charles could identify James Brown in the dark, and not just because Mr. Charles was blind. I don't know how he did it. I was walking down a hall one day and he happened to pass me and suddenly he broke into a big smile and said, "That's that James Brown. . . . 'Please Please Please' James Brown, isn't it?"

He said it in such a nice way that I couldn't help breaking into a chuckle. "Yeah, that's me, Mr. Charles."

We became such good friends after that. The last time I saw Brother Ray was not too long ago, in the Hamptons. We were talking before a show, and I told him the same thing I feel now—that he never got what he deserved: the proper respect or the accolades due him. He never was able to achieve what he wanted, which was to be a central player in the world of popular music. I'm not saying that he didn't make it large. It's just that a man of the genius and stature of Ray Charles should have been honored and respected much more than he was for his abilities and his contributions. I think he was a little bitter about that and I don't blame him one bit.

One of the biggest differences about our styles is that he kept strictly to the music. That was all he was interested in. You never saw his name connected to politics or the civil rights movement the way you did mine. He didn't have that kind of personality, and maybe that's why people didn't give him the recognition he deserved. I hate it when people say *just* a musician, as if that's not enough in this man's world. Conversely, maybe I would have gone farther as a musician if I weren't so preoccupied with helping others, especially children. No matter how you look at it, it's a trade-off, one way or the other.

His recent death is a deep loss to me, personally, and to the world. His music remains part of the living cultural legacy of twentieth-century America. Rest in peace, Brother Ray. We will never forget you.

Please Please Please" was always my most popular song, and it never failed to drive the audiences crazy! I'd come out at the top of the show, politely introduce myself by saying, "I'm James Brown, these are the Flames, and we made this song." Then I'd explode into a thirty-five-, forty-minute rendition of it, with Danny Ray serving as my "Cape Man," a job he performs to this day.

The song is really like a movie that could take place in the church of any man's wounded heart. Black people have a special tendency to let love hang, to put it out there, to plead their case on their hands and knees when they are wounded in love. At least on one level, "Please Please

Please" is about a man begging his woman to take him back because he loves her so. He drops to his knees and literally begs for mercy. When he gets none, he slowly gets up, turns his back to the world, and limps toward the darkness. For comfort, a friend appears and drapes over him the cape of mourning, to protect him, to keep him warm, to console him. Just as it appears that all hope is lost, the man throws his cape off of his shoulders, turns his face back to the audience—to life, really—goes to the front of the stage, and once again pleads to the love of his life. I was that man, and Danny Ray was my comforter. Each time I threw that cape off, the audiences would get wilder and wilder. The ritual of the cape act became a stage drama that was part religious expiation, romantic crisis, and ultimate boxing match in the arena of love.

While the song worked beautifully onstage, it was quite another thing to capture all of that on a three-minute record. I remember the night I laid the track for Mr. Syd Nathan for King Records, and how worried he was that I was losing my mind. "James Brown is crazy," he kept telling anyone who would listen. I was already writing my own material—most performers during this period of time sang songs that others wrote. Everyone had a specialty— the songwriter, the arranger, the producer, the performer. Slowly but surely, I was taking over all of these roles, something that was completely unheard of in those times. That was all bad enough to Mr. Nathan—but who, he wondered, was going to play over and over again a record that repeated one word so many times? Where's the rest of the song?

He asked me to change the lyrics more than once, but I knew something he didn't. I knew what was inside of me, and how it needed to come out, with all its many repetitions. It was exactly the way it needed to be. Some of it came, no doubt, from my gospel upbringing, and some of it came from the music I'd heard as a child, like that Louis Jordan and his Tympany Five, from Tucson, Arizona. I used to watch Jordan in the movies, playing his saxophone with a six-piece band, all in what looked like some cramped uptown apartment. What killed me was when I found out he was not only the sax player, but the writer, producer, and arranger as well. His songs were filled with stories and fanciful tales, mostly about women, and shrieks and stomps and abrupt rhythmic changes, and tightly choreographed jumps and moves. His stuff was, in many ways, the true precursor to what young Black performers today call rap music. What really got to me was the link between music and women.

That's when I first learned that singing was about style, romance, and delivery, not just about words and music. I took a lot from Louis Jordan, and hoped to model myself in his image, because in my mind, he was the best. His talent was so awesome I thought it had to be supernatural.

The connection between us was the context of our

performance—his little apartment and my stage were the same, both dressed with a beautiful if unattainable vision of female perfection. That was the common inspiration I shared with Louis Jordan.

But sometimes a songwriter can get his inspiration a million miles from his immediate surroundings, real or staged. Cole Porter, that urban, sophisticated songwriter of the thirties, had a huge hit with "Don't Fence Me In," a song everyone thought had to have been written by an Oklahoma cowboy. Who knows where his inspiration came from for that? But it was real, it was genuine, and it worked. Mine, like Louis Jordan's, came from somewhere a little closer to home, a place deep inside of me, my *soul,* the powerful and at times metaphysical connection to my heart that flows directly to the last row in the balcony. That is what soul is, heart singing, and that was what "Please Please Please" was all about.

After the first few thousand copies of "Please Please Please" were sold, Mr. Nathan officially changed the group's billing to James Brown *with* the Famous Flames, then soon after, James Brown *and* the Famous Flames. That's when some of the first real troubles with the group began. Everything then exploded one day when the boys came in to rehearse and found that Mr. Nathan and I had decided to change the name of the group to James Brown and *His* Famous Flames. I felt I deserved that much. After all, I was the one writing the music, doing the lead singing, and bringing people in to fill the seats. I was the attraction, and we wanted to make sure that the audience knew what it was getting. I understood the others were sore, but they weren't the stars of the show. The profession we were in was called show *business*, and our billing had to reflect our bestselling product, which happened to be James Brown.

What's more, it felt like I was doing 95 percent of the work. I was designing the stage show, writing the songs, working out the choreography, directing the lights, playing keyboards, and really overlaying the show with my personality. And that's the simple, hard truth of the matter. I knew it hurt Mr. Byrd more than the others, because he had discovered me. But "Bobby Byrd" had not become a household name. And "Bobby Byrd" did not sell our records or the tickets to our shows. And he knew it. When the trouble within the group started, and a lot of feelings were hurt—especially his—Mr. Byrd, to his credit, hung in there and tried to keep us together, and I will always applaud him for being a man that way.

But there's no way around it: the girls went for James Brown, girls told their boyfriends who they wanted to see, their boyfriends bought the tickets—and that was our bread and butter.

More often than not, because our venues were still so intimate, the stage nothing more than the corner of a dance floor, women would often find themselves close enough to the stage, hysterical, and once or twice one of them was able to actually grab me. There was one time I'll never forget, in a club in Alabama, when this big Black woman jumped right on top of me. She had long nails as sharp as razors and she nearly cut my throat from ear to ear she was so excited!

Whenever a group starts to experience success, inevitably, changes take place, both onstage and off. Promoters come to see you, record labels send scouts, and the truth of the matter is, if you stand still, you start to slide. Growth means upward mobility, and that was the only direction I was interested in. Somewhere along the way, while playing the endless clubs and music joints that peppered the South, I happened to meet a big-time promoter by the name of Ben Bart. He was a large brown-haired man with white sideburns who managed such legendary acts as Hank Ballard as well as the Five Royals. Ballard's hits included "Annie Had a Baby," "Sexy Ways," and "The Twist." Even before I met Mr. Bart, Hank Ballard had been another major stylistic influence on me. When we did finally get together, I was impressed with Mr. Bart's show business know-how. After only a few minutes together, I knew deep inside that he was going to replace Mr. Nathan on my show business journey.

Professionally, I knew that sooner or later I needed to

make a change. It wasn't that I didn't like Mr. Nathan. It was more along the lines that he didn't always understand what I was trying to do. In the beginning I may not have gotten paid all that much, but I was learning, gaining knowledge from him of how the business worked, and crucially, allowed to keep my own copyrights. Mr. Nathan wanted me to have the opportunity to invest in my own talent. For those reasons I will always be grateful to him to the end of my days. But still, my creativity had out-paced the vision, such as it was, of King Records, and be-cause of it, my days with the label and with Mr. Nathan were numbered.

If that sounds a little cold, well, let me tell you a story about managers. First of all, they are very difficult to find, especially if they're honest. Somewhere along the line early on, I worked briefly with the notorious Morris Levy, who never liked to pay anybody anything. One time I was over at his office and I asked him to give me some of the money due me. He patted me on the back, he played pool with me, and at the end of the day, he gave me this tiny color TV, a new portable model that nobody as yet had. See, he said, look what a good guy I am. I took it, went home, and a couple of days later I came back and told him I still wanted my money. He got very angry and said okay, but first I had to return the TV set. "Don't worry," I said, smiling. "I have it right here." I reached in and took it out of my jacket pocket! I didn't want toys. I wasn't a child. I wanted the money I had rightfully earned. After all, I was the Hardest-Working Man in Show Business!

You would be amazed at how many managers think a TV will be a good substitute for bread and butter and a roof over your head, food and lodging that you have the right to, while they live in big mansions scheming how to keep what doesn't belong to them. Not all managers, of course, and not Mr. Nathan, but in the early days of rock and roll, there were quite a few.

I first came across Mr. Bart while we were on tour with some of the Motown acts, all of us getting more and more television exposure. We had already done Dick Clark's *American Bandstand* and the Black TV syndicated show *Soul Train*. As it happened, a lot of the Motown acts played the same cities that I did, and on the nights they were dark, they'd come over and see what we were doing. That's when I first met the Temptations, the Supremes, the Miracles, Marvin Gaye, Mary Wells, and the great Jackie Wilson, who was on the Brunswick label and had gotten into the music business after an unsuccessful career as a boxer with his friend Berry Gordy, who wrote Jackie's first hit "Reet Petite" and would go on to create the Motown label and the Motown sound.

Speaking of Mr. Gordy, he was like every other manager I had ever encountered, from Morris Levy on up. It didn't seem to bother him that I already had a manager. He sensed I was growing increasingly unhappy with Mr. Nathan, and suggested that I simply get rid of him and join Motown under his personal supervision. He tried to convince me by telling me that I could surely sell more records with his huge label than with Mr. Nathan's tiny King Records.

I thought about it, but knew I could never exist happily on Motown. His acts were a little too soft for me: too much pop, not enough soul. I was still way too raw for the kind of polished music they were willing to do. For instance, they had their choreography, which was great, but it was too rehearsed, down to the last toe-step. Mine was different, spontaneous, and no two nights the same. Mine didn't come from a rehearsal hall—it came from my heart and soul, and there was no way I was ever going to change that, for Motown or anywhere else.

Another thing was the sound of Motown itself. The first thing Mr. Gordy did to make sure he had hit records was to cut the bass out of all the singles so they would sound good on AM car radios, which was pretty much the only way kids heard music in those days—when they drove. I couldn't believe that! To me, the bass was like the heartbeat, the essence of the rhythm, the place where the flow of any song comes from. As a result, for me a lot of Motown sounded a little too slick, too happy, too high school. Not that they didn't have some great ones, among the greatest being Junior Walker, who went as far as Motown could take him. I loved him and all the rest of the talent at the label, but I knew I could never be part of what they were in to. Under Mr. Gordy's strict, hands-on direction, the Motown show and catalogue were shaped around pop, and their acts were made to strut like minstrels. They were like the caviar of Black music, while I, on the other hand, was strictly soul food.

Shortly after my tour with the Motown groups ended, I made the big switch. Mr. Nathan was out and Mr. Bart was in. He promised to take me to the big time, and the next thing I knew, we arrived in New York City. It was my first time ever in the so-called Big Apple and I had never seen anything like it. First chance I got I went straight uptown, to Harlem and the Apollo, a few days before we were scheduled to play there ourselves. I knew as soon as I walked through the front doors of the sacred temple of soul that I was entering some kind of shrine to Black music, a place as important to the history of my people as the Museum of Natural History two miles to the south was to the rest of the world.

The first show I saw there was with the Dells and the Cadillacs, who did their great "Speedo" routine onstage that took them right through the audience and out the front door onto the street! Amazing!

After the show, I went backstage to say hello to some of the boys, and met the Dominoes, who were due to come in after the Dells and the Cadillacs for a solid week. The Dominoes had begun as a gospel group, but when they made the switch to R & B and then pop, they added a succession of singers, including Clyde McPhatter and Jackie Wilson. I knew a lot of the newer boys in the group because they had at one time or another been on the King label and personally handled by Mr. Nathan.

We spent some time together with them, and I listened to all that Billy Ward, the lead singer of the Dominoes, had to say about his time on King. It was a familiar story, and enough to make me feel good about my decision to go with Mr. Bart. Despite the fact that I had officially left King Records and Mr. Nathan, some of the others in the group thought I was making a big mistake. Their inability to see what I was trying to do proved to be the final nail in our coffin, and shortly thereafter, with Mr. Bart's enthusiastic support, I decided the time had come for me to split from the Flames and become a solo performer.

Too many riffs over everything from billing to money, to management, to spotlights had come between us. And of course, there was the issue of how to live. The other boys were either starting to get that feeling on their own or were being pressured by their women to get off the road and settle down, and that kind of talk didn't sit well with me. As far as I was concerned, we *were* settled, in a life of performing that we had worked so hard to have. But I couldn't make them see the future as anything different from the

present, and because of it, there were too many resent-
ments between us. Sad as it made me, I knew the end had
come, even as we had reached the pinnacle: New York
City and the great Apollo Theater.

Ironically, the first thing Mr. Bart did was to put me on
tour with, of all people, Little Richard, something that I
was less than thrilled about. Old sensitivities still lurked
beneath our bright and shiny costumes. I'll never know
why some things happened when and how they did. But as
it turned out, this particular pairing would be quite fortu-
itous for me. Early on in the tour, one night without warning, Little Richard suddenly announced to the world that
he was retiring from rock and roll to pursue a life of gospel
music and religious devotion. He was a star solo act, and
because of his decision, Mr. Bart moved me into his slot
on the dozens of already booked dates still to come in
many of the country's best venues. As it turned out, the
Dominoes were booked on a lot of those bills, so for me it
was, in a way, like touring with the old Flames. I liked it so
much I decided to re-form the group, this time strictly as a
backup instrument-playing set of musicians, keeping the
name and replacing those originals I didn't want or who
didn't want to come back of their own accord. I also
agreed to return to King Records to complete my recording contract with Mr. Nathan, while maintaining Mr. Bart
as my manager. All of this moving and switching kept me

pretty busy until the middle of 1958, when all my touring and recording obligations were finally completed.

One of the last records I did on King was in March 1958, and it turned out to be one of the biggest of my entire career—*Try Me*, which exploded onto the R & B charts at number one, so strong that it landed me on the pop charts for the first time, at #48. It was a song in the familiar James Brown style: on one level a love song; on another a plea filled with courtesy, respect, and a bit of a request for the audience to try out my wares by sampling my music. Give *me* a shot, please! Try *me*. That was what the song was really saying.

I'll never forget receiving the biggest royalty check for a single in my career. "Please Please Please" did well, but that had taken time to build. I got the check for "Try Me" while I was in Charleston, South Carolina. Although I had had hits before, this time it was for a solo recording, and under a new manager, and the amount blew me away. *$3600!* And it was only the beginning. Before 1958 was over, "Try Me" had taken off into the stratosphere and became the number-one ballad *all over the world!*

In April of 1959, on the strength of "Try Me," Mr. Bart got me booked for the first time as a solo act at the Apollo. This was, to me, the highest honor there was.

The show's star headliner was Little Willie John. I was appearing on the rest of the bill with the Upsetters, the comedy act of Butterbeans and Susie, Verna White, the

Senators, and Vi Kemp. Now Little Willie, who was a dear friend of mine, was nobody's fool. He knew the kind of power my performance contained, and so he put me toward the front of the bill to give himself and the audience enough breathing room before he came out. Sure enough, the audiences went crazy when the new Flames and I took the stage, and it didn't take long before Frank Schiffman, the owner of the Apollo, began talking about how he wanted to move us to the back end of the bill. However, it didn't happen, even though it became increasingly obvious that that was where we belonged. One night in the middle of our run, in a fit of frustration and disgust I told the boys to simply pack up their instruments, because we were leaving. Panicked, Mr. Schiffman begged me to tell him what was wrong, and I did. When I was finished, he smiled and said, "Is that all? From now on, James Brown costars and goes on right before Mr. Willie John."

I went into orbit! I couldn't believe my luck. And sure enough, after that, everything else began to fall into place. Now all the biggest theaters on the circuit wanted me. My final night at the Apollo was a killer, and the audience let us know it.

Back at my hotel, as I was packing for the drive down to our next stop, Washington, I heard a knock at the door. I had no idea who it was, maybe some girl or the management sending up flowers. I really didn't think about it too much and said, "Come in," not bothering to look up from my suitcase. What happened next still sends shivers up and down my spine, as cold and as hair-raising as the night when it first occurred. I heard the door open; then someone step into the room. I waited, still not looking up, listening for what they had to say. When the silence continued, I finally turned around, and there standing before me was my mother, who I hadn't seen or heard from for twenty years.

I didn't know what to say or do. My heart was racing. My brain was burning. My soul was on fire. Twenty years dissolved in that moment—I was standing there looking at my past. More as a defense than anything else, I suddenly broke into a smile. "Hey, I been looking for you for a long time," I said. That wasn't really true, but I didn't know what else I could say, besides "Were you looking for me as well?" It burned a little bit because I knew I wasn't too hard to find. She smiled back, and I could see she had no teeth left in her mouth.

"I'm glad to see you," she said softly. Those words hung in the air like bad cooking.

Was she glad to see me? I wondered. More to the point, was I glad to see her? I have to say in all honesty that I wasn't sure. I'm still not. So many things ran through my head all at once. It was true that I had missed her so much, that I had wanted her to be there for all the good times, including my wedding day, but she hadn't been. And it was true that she had abandoned me when times were rough and she found what she thought was a better life for herself without me. Yet now that I was a star she had come back to me.

Why? I wondered. What did she want? Was it money? Was it forgiveness? Was it both? Neither? I stared deep into her eyes looking for answers, but found only tears. They said a lot, only they didn't tell me anything. Most important, I couldn't find a way to let her back in. She had closed a door in my life that I could never fully reopen.

We talked. I don't remember about what—they were just words filling up the space between us. What I do know is that it all seemed too late to me. I didn't see her much again after that strange and awkward night but I still remember the power of that moment that remains to this day, one of the most difficult and gut-wrenching of my entire life.

Try me. . . .

FIVE

I N 1963 I FORMED MY OWN PRODUCTION COMPANY WITH the only person I felt I could totally trust—my daddy. Not long after, I remember someone asking him, "Hey, Joe Brown, ain't you glad your son's singing and not fighting anymore?"

"No," he said. "I'm glad he *sung!*" I knew what he meant. He meant the choice, not the activity, that I became some*body*, and that I did it on my own, without his approval or guidance. It meant a lot to him that I made a choice to be a performer and that I was brave enough to give it a shot. It didn't matter as much whether or not I succeeded or failed, just that I had the courage to try to carve out a better life for myself, one poor Black boy brave enough to walk into the rich White man's world with his head held high.

That was the way he thought, and even though, like me, he didn't have any education, he had something perhaps even more valuable to give me—a sharp, common street sense. "Better to die on your feet than live on your knees," he used to tell me, as far back as I can remember. I still believe that, and brother, that may be why I'm still standing. I told my own kids the same types of things as soon as they were old enough to understand what I was saying. If they wanted to do something, whether it be music, business, or any other venture of value to them, they were going to have to learn how to fight for it to get their fair share. That was the way it was when my father was growing up, that's the way it was when I was growing up, and to a large extent, that's the way it still is.

Back in the early days of R & B, rock-a-soul, and rock and roll, performers never made any real money off their music, primarily because of the way the business was set up. It was essentially a nickel, dime, and quarter cash machine—the jukeboxes were the banks, and the old 45 RPM records were sold for cash out of the back trunks of cars to the local record shops. Personal appearances by the artists were all paid for in cash, and publishing was where the only real money was. No one even knew what publishing rights were!

Because of it, lots of performers took a financial beat-

ing, including many of the great musical pioneers, such as
B. B. King, Chuck Berry, Bo Diddley, and Little Richard,
just to name a few. And a lot of the so-called media heroes, including the DJs—the trusted parent-substitute
"friends" of the teenagers who claimed to "understand kids
the way their folks didn't"—were the biggest rip-off artists.
They'd hire us to play shows at the holidays, eight or nine
continual rotations, around the clock, with a cheap movie
in between, pulling in millions at the box office and paying
us next to nothing for it.

Our music had proved that it could produce lots of
money. The problem was, that money went into everybody's pocket but those of the performers. At the time, it
was believed that the DJs—those men on the radio who
played their so-called "favorite" records—were the heroes
because they got our songs out to the kids. In fact, that
wasn't always the case. Most of them were hustlers like
everyone else in the business. They found ways to cash in
that eventually cost most of them their livelihoods and, in
some cases, their freedom. This all came down during the
payola scandals of the late fifties.

Payola is one of the most misunderstood chapters in the
history of rock and roll. It really had less to do with payoffs
than with race. Independent records posed a major threat
to the big labels and, therefore, had to be eliminated. The
so-called "majors" were slow to come to rock and roll and
waited until their bottom lines shrank to do something

about it. By then, of course, rock and roll had become a cultural phenomenon, and was not that easy to get rid of. What they needed was a reason to outlaw the music. What they found was twofold. For the public, the rationale was greed, thievery, illegal payoffs, a way to influence public opinion. One congressman went so far as to say that this music had to come with payoffs because it was so awful no one would play it otherwise.

But the private reason was much more powerful and insidious. The real fear that the majors played on was the social one. Allow your White daughters to listen to Black rock and roll today, and tomorrow, they will be giving birth to Black babies. Payola was nothing less than a Congressional purge meant to eliminate the growing popularity of Black music from the social consciousness.

This strategy worked because the sacred cows of rock and roll—the DJs—were in fact vulnerable to the charges of payola. They did put their names down as coauthors on a lot of the music they played. And they did take money under the table. It wasn't illegal at the time, but it did compromise their avowed pure love of the music that they played.

Alan Freed, the most popular DJ at the time, is the one who usually gets all the blame for this because his name suspiciously appeared on the copyrights of several Chuck Berry recordings (and other acts as well) as coauthor. That meant he was entitled to a part of the royalties. Not so coincidentally, many of those songs also became the most played on his radio show.

I don't blame Mr. Freed for anything he did, or had to do. He had given a generation an anchor to hang the concept of "rock and roll" on with his radio broadcasts and live shows. And the truth is, whether we want to believe it or not, without him, none of us would have gone very far. Little Richard was singing gospel-tinged rock and roll. Chuck Berry was doing some variation of country-infused rock. I was doing R & B and soul. But under the umbrella of Alan Freed, to the listeners it all became more or less the same thing: rock and roll. He took a lot of different voices of the pop culture and brought them together on one wavelength, out of which came a stronger sense of sound that couldn't have been accomplished by the artists individually. And that just can't be overlooked.

The tragedy of all of this was that he became the focus of the scandal, and its ultimate victim. Others had done a lot worse, and made far more money, but Alan Freed, who, false rumor had it, was part Black, lost everything he had and died just a few years later, not only broke but a broken man.

I felt bad for Alan when he died. He reminded me of Stephen Foster, another pioneer who changed the notion of what popular music was, but who never made any money off his own songs. Stephen Foster died with seven cents in his pocket. Bill Robinson, the great Black dancer who costarred with Shirley Temple in those movies, died with even less than that, and honestly I don't believe Alan Freed had much more when he passed.

Whenever any of us complained back in those days, the men with the money or the power would say, "Yes, you're right. I know. I understand, but that's the way it is." *That's the way it is?* That's like saying, "God is the Devil!" *That's the way it was because they were able to make it that way.* All I could think of when I learned Alan Freed was dead and that he had died unwilling to admit that he had done anything wrong—and because of it, was never able to work again—was the words my father had told me: *Better to die on your feet than live on your knees.*

All I wanted was to make music and deliver the good feelings it produced in my fans. After payola, I started thinking about how money represents the system, the machine, and ultimately, the music, while the men who make it represent only their feelings. So we have created a world that has to pit Man against the Machine. The people who are the inventors in this system often think more about the machine than the people it will be used for—or against. On the positive side, the machine was invented to make life easier, and for those who controlled it—for those with the money—it presented a better life all around. Look at the law—money buys the machine that buys freedom. Medicine: money buys the care that brings the cure. Food:

money buys the best meal that keeps you healthiest. Women: money provides the best life for those who look the youngest and the most beautiful.

Youth is the crucial factor. Most people over forty-five who aren't established have nothing to look forward to. If they don't have significant money by then, everything falls to the wayside of their lives. When they get old and they need the essentials to keep them living, they can't afford them and they die. Old age simply costs too much to keep people alive when they get there, at least in this country. We have no plan to keep them going—we have no interest because there's no money in it.

This is the way it is and always has been. And when I found myself making it in the world of music, I determined that the only effective defense against payola, getting ripped off, or being pushed aside by the next generation was to start my own machine. To do so, I had to start my own record company. I was intent on taking control of my destiny. The only way I could continue to be a success was to be the biggest success in the world. If I was going to be a failure, then at least I would fail honestly and not because some smooth dude had ripped me off right in front of my own eyes. And that is why I decided to start my own company, Fair Deal Productions.

I chose that name to make a statement about how I felt the music business should operate. I wanted to say that from now on this was the way things were going to be, if

James Brown had something to do with it. I wasn't going to be one more "nigger bum," as I heard White music execs refer to the Black acts who were forever coming around begging for food money. I was going to do things a little differently, no matter what it took. I knew I was going to need not just good help, but the best in the business. That's when I met up with a man by the name of Marty Machat, who happened to be the lawyer for the Rolling Stones. Mr. Machat was instrumental in helping Daddy and me put Fair Deal Productions together.

Mr. Machat came along at a time when my contract had run out with King Records. Mr. Machat then signed me, through Fair Deal, to Mercury Records' so-called "race" division, Mercury/Smash, located in New York City. And even while lawsuits flew back and forth between Mr. Nathan and Mr. Machat over the last remaining obstacle to my freedom—who had the publishing rights to my music and me, something that felt a little too close like slave auctioning as far as I was concerned—I turned all my attention to what I did best: making music.

The first tune I recorded for Smash was "I'm Just a Nobody," in the spring of '63, followed by a duet with Anna King, "Baby, Baby, Baby," in March '64. Then a month later, my solo version of "Caldonia" was released. It was a song I had been performing on and off since the Cremona Trio days. All the while, Mr. Nathan kept recycling old James Brown product on King, including another go-round with "Please Please Please" and "Again." I wasn't happy about this, as it was flooding the market with too much of my music at the same time, forcing me into competition with myself.

As it happened, "Please Please Please" eventually made more money for me than any of my other records, and more than a lot of my records *combined*! At the time, though, I was eager to make my deal at Smash a good one, and to save up enough money to buy a new and bigger house in the great New York City for Velma and me.

Looking back now, the truth of the matter is that I really didn't want to move to New York City at all. I had been perfectly happy living in Macon. There, I had a Black manager, I was involved with Southern Black culture, and I was constantly trying to help kids get into Black colleges by performing benefits for them—those sorts of things. The move to New York City was really a necessity to hold on to the reins of power over the very machine that I myself had created.

It was a rough ride. The demands of the business were such that the big music companies—and of course, the Apollo, in which I was playing more and more—were all in New York City, so I thought I had to be there too. Hang with the big guns and you become a big gun.

I bought a large house in Queens, not knowing it was not the center of the city, or anywhere near Harlem. It was a mostly White neighborhood that we were moving into.

In truth, I knew very little about New York, other than 125th Street. I might as well have stayed in Macon. I was close to only a few people in the industry, but what people! One of them was Count Basie, who, I discovered, was also a neighbor to one of my all-time heroes, the great Joe Louis, who lived only a couple of doors down from the both of us. Other then those cats, I rarely saw or spoke to anyone else on my block, or in my neighborhood, or in the entire borough of Queens. Not because I didn't want to—it was the strangest thing. In this, the biggest city in the world, no one seemed to know, or want to get to know, anybody else.

The first thing I did after moving in was to paint and renovate the entire place to bring it up to my speed. I settled on a gray-and-black motif for the colors of the exterior. I was never sure why I chose that particular scheme, except that maybe it was a reflection of how I felt inside at the time, down in the gray area of my soul, where I was increasingly surrounded by an even darker blackness. It was an interesting time, not helped by my new and very strange surroundings.

That June I cut my second single for Smash Records, "Out of Sight" and it went through the roof. I would have to say that "Out of Sight" was the first song I had written that was a little different from the standard-type tunes I had been cranking out. Everything about it was new—the rhythm, the arrangement, the lyrics, and the

The incomparable Godfather of Soul, James Brown. © LYNN GOLDSMITH/CORBIS

James Brown's father, Joe Brown, was forced to leave his son to serve in the Navy.
FROM THE COLLECTION OF THE AUTHOR

Susie Brown, James' mother, left the family when James was only four years old.
FROM THE COLLECTION OF THE AUTHOR

James Brown in the early years of his career.
FROM THE COLLECTION OF THE AUTHOR

Alto Reform School in Toccoa, Georgia, where James Brown was incarcerated at sixteen. While there, he was visited by gospel singer Bobby Byrd. FROM THE COLLECTION OF THE AUTHOR

The original members of the Famous Flames, prior to Brown joining the band: (left to right) Bobby Byrd, Nash Knox, Sylvester Keels, Johnny Terry, and (with guitar) Nayfloyd Scott. FROM THE COLLECTION OF THE AUTHOR

James Brown leading a rehearsal session in the sixties. FROM THE COLLECTION OF THE AUTHOR

James Brown and the Famous Flames. Bobby Byrd is at center.
FROM THE COLLECTION OF THE AUTHOR

The James Brown Revue performing at a concert in the mid-sixties along with the great R & B singers of the time. James is backed by the Famous Flames.
FROM THE COLLECTION OF THE AUTHOR

A collection of posters and show bills from Brown's performances in the sixties. FROM THE COLLECTION OF THE AUTHOR

The old Ritz Theater, now the Schaefer Center, in Toccoa, Georgia—the site of many of James Brown's early performances. The door on the right was for Blacks only, and it led directly to the balcony. Whites entered through the middle doors. FROM THE COLLECTION OF THE AUTHOR

Velma Warren Brown, James'
first wife.

FROM THE COLLECTION OF THE AUTHOR

As a boy, James Brown used to
shine shoes for nickels in front
of the radio station WRDW in
Augusta, Georgia. Years later, he
owned the station, one of many
he acquired in the late sixties.

FROM THE COLLECTION OF THE AUTHOR

The impeccable James Brown.

FROM THE COLLECTION OF THE AUTHOR

James Brown appearing with Hubert Humphrey in front of the Watts Labor Community Action Committee in 1968. Humphrey was helpful in getting Brown the okay to go to Vietnam to perform for U.S. troops. © BETTMAN/CORBIS

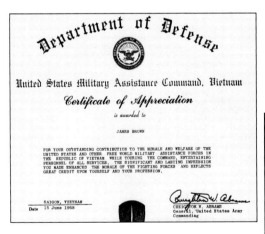

Accolades awarded to James Brown in appreciation of his efforts in entertaining and boosting the morale of U.S. troops in Vietnam: (above) a certificate of appreciation presented to Brown by General Creighton W. Abrams; (right) a plaque awarded to Brown by the Chicago Vietnam Veterans Parade Committee. FROM THE COLLECTION OF THE AUTHOR

By 1969, James Brown was cemented as a cultural icon, appearing here on a collectible trading stamp.

© TED STRESHINSKY/CORBIS

Some candid photos of James Brown and his father, Joe.

FROM THE COLLECTION OF THE AUTHOR

Brown's second wife, Deidre Jenkins Brown, with daughters (clockwise from top) Yamma, Deana, and Venisha. FROM THE COLLECTION OF THE AUTHOR

James Brown with his third wife, Adrianne.
FROM THE COLLECTION OF THE AUTHOR

James Brown's son Teddy, who died tragically in an auto accident. FROM THE COLLECTION OF THE AUTHOR

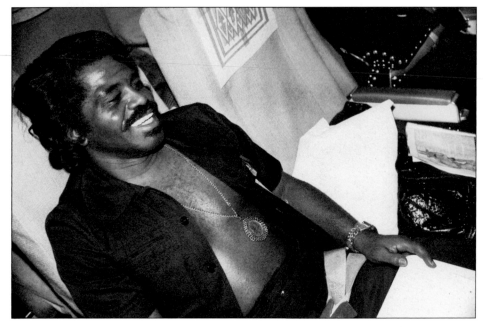

James Brown flying to Africa for a string of concerts and to see the Ali-Foreman fight. Brown was one of the first performers—Black or White—to own a private jet to help him keep up with his demanding tour schedule. © LYNN GOLDSMITH/CORBIS

James Brown and Muhammad Ali. © LYNN GOLDSMITH/CORBIS

James Brown leaving it all on-stage during a performance in the seventies.

© LYNN GOLDSMITH/CORBIS

James Brown has always been one of the great leaders championing the Black cause: with the Reverend Al Sharpton in the early eighties (left) and being commended by Malcolm X's widow, Betty Shabazz, at a ceremony in 1992 (below).

SHARPTON PHOTO © LYNN GOLDSMITH/CORBIS;

SHABAZZ PHOTO © JOHN VAN HASSELT/CORBIS SYGMA

Throughout his career, James Brown was able to leave an impression on many presidents and political dignitaries, including (clockwise from top left) Hubert Humphrey, Richard Nixon, Ronald Reagan, Colin Powell, and George W. Bush, among many others.

POWELL PHOTO © ROBERT TRIPPETT/POOL/CORBIS. ALL OTHER PHOTOS FROM THE COLLECTION OF THE AUTHOR

James Brown with his star on the Walk of Fame in Hollywood, California. © PACHA/CORBIS

James Brown addresses the crowd at the opening of the James Brown Soul Center.
© WAMPLER GAYLON/CORBIS SYGMA

James Brown and his music have had a profound impact on the lives and art of many fellow musicians. Here with (clockwise from top left) Ozzy Osbourne, Ron Wood from the Rolling Stones, Lenny Kravitz, Michael Jackson, and Paul McCartney (foreground) and Brian Wilson.

KRAVITZ, JACKSON, AND McCARTNEY AND WILSON PHOTOS © REUTERS/ CORBIS. ALL OTHER PHOTOS FROM THE COLLECTION OF THE AUTHOR

James Brown and long-time friend and personal manager, Charles Bobbit.

FROM THE COLLECTION OF THE AUTHOR

James Brown reuniting with Bobby Byrd, DJ Big Sol, and old bandmates at a meeting with the Honorable C. Jack Ellis, the first Black mayor of Macon, Georgia. Big Sol recorded Brown and the Famous Flames' "Please Please Please" just to get it on the air. Later, it was recorded professionally at King Records in Cincinnati, and became a gigantic hit for Brown, launching his music career. To the right of Brown are the Honorable C. Jack Ellis, Big Sol, and Bobby Byrd.

FROM THE COLLECTION OF THE AUTHOR

James Brown with his wife, Tomi Rae Brown, receiving the prestigious Kennedy Center Honor for his lifetime contribution to the arts, on December 7, 2003, in Washington, D.C.

FROM THE COLLECTION OF THE AUTHOR

As long as the fire still burns in his heart, James Brown will continue to wow audiences worldwide. Here he is performing his trademark cape drama with longtime MC, Danny Ray.

FROM THE COLLECTION OF THE AUTHOR

way the beat kept on jerking up and hitting. It broke all the rules of three-minute hits, yet still proved a smash, sort of like leading with your right when you're fighting and somehow knocking the other guy out anyway. It's something everybody tells you never to do in the ring until you win the fight and you suddenly become the best fighter who ever lived.

After that, in November of 1964, I was on my way to California to appear in what they called the TAMI Show, which was to prove my breakthrough to the other, Whiter side of the rock-and-roll universe. I decided to do TAMI against the advice of a lot of people I trusted in those days, who almost to a man told me not to dare to even think about it. They believed that I was reaching beyond my limits, and that even though the show was supposedly integrated, with a lot of Motown acts like the Supremes, Marvin Gaye, and Smokey Robinson and the Miracles, they were all essentially softer pop-type groups. The real stars of the show were the White middle-class America of Surfin' City USA, which was not quite ready to go one-on-one with the deep soul music of James Brown.

Me being me, and maybe even *because* of that, I went anyway.

The show was innovative in more ways than one. For instance, it was kinescoped, or recorded on film directly off of the television cameras set up at the Santa Monica Civic High School auditorium, which is about a mile from the beautiful Pacific Ocean. It was later intended for viewing in movie theaters all across the country. This was a highly innovative experiment in what would one day become part of the mass-media marketing of rock and roll.

We arrived at the theater early in the day to take part in the rehearsals. Because there were TV cameras, everything had to be precisely staged so the director could follow the action. That meant live rock and roll, and in those days the cameras were big and bulky, so good technical coordination was key to capturing a great performance for broadcast.

There were also quite a few of the British Invasion acts on the show, those who had hit it big in the wake of the Beatles, who had themselves become an instant phenomenon in America earlier that same year in January, after they appeared on Mr. Ed Sullivan's Sunday night television institution. The Rolling Stones and Gerry and the Pacemakers were among them. Gerry Marsden of the Pacemakers was very friendly at rehearsals, open and glad-handing, always polite to me with a big smile on his face, which I appreciated. The Stones, on the other hand, were already leading the lives of superstars, even though they perhaps hadn't quite as yet earned that right. When they arrived at the auditorium, they went straight to their dressing room, locked the doors, and refused to see anyone until it was time for them to rehearse their set.

When it was my turn to go on, I hit the stage on fire, just

because I was told by so many people not to push my heat button too hard. I mean, I torched those songs, and as I did so, I could see out of the corner of my eye the other performers on the program had begun to gather around in the wings to watch me do my thing. I'm sure the likes of the very pale Lesley Gore, the loveliest of the young female pop performers on the bill, had never seen anything like "Please Please Please" before.

Soon enough, word reached the Stones back in their dressing room that something was happening on the stage that they had better check out.

There had, in fact, been some talk earlier that day of the order of the show being reversed but Steve Binder, the director, would have none of it. The Stones were the jewel of the show, he insisted, and he wasn't going to deny them their right to close, James Brown or no James Brown.

So we went on as scheduled, and the minute we kicked in with our opening number, "Out of Sight," all those White kids in the audience went crazy! I mean they jumped out of their seats and raised their hands over their heads and screamed their heads off! They knew nothing about soul music—that much was obvious to me, not only from them, but from the rest of the show. This was the first time anybody in that neck of the woods had got a dose of real soul, James Brown–style.

When I got to "Please Please Please," I was in full stride. They understood immediately what the message was. I was, as always, extremely polite and well-mannered, and I'd even go so far as to say humble, as I asked the most important question of my life, and maybe for some of them as well. I was trying to teach them about my world, my music, my life, without shoving it down anybody's throat.

As I sang "Please Please Please," I remember that Mick Jagger quietly came to the lip of the wing and watched intently as I did twenty-five minutes or so of this blistering rendition, complete with cape, knee falls, and all the vocal calisthenics I was capable of. I was told afterward that Mr. Jagger went through a complete pack of cigarettes before I was through, and was so stunned by what he saw that he wanted to get his band's set changed, and have another act put on first so that they wouldn't have to immediately follow me. Because they *couldn't* follow me. Can you imagine it? They were supposed to be the headliners of this great cast of young rock and rollers, the closers, an honor meant for the biggest act of the night. Mr. Jagger, though, learned that night *it was not so easy to follow James Brown!*

SIX

I ALWAYS LOVED FAMILY LIFE, AND TRIED TO FOLLOW ITS traditions as carefully as I could, although certain traditions meant more to me than others. Holidays, for one thing. My favorite is and has always been Thanksgiving, because it isn't about buying things and giving things and supporting a big-business industry built on faked affection. It's about getting the family together, everyone sitting down to eat, counting up our personal blessings, and being grateful for living in America. I have always especially loved spending time with my kids on holidays, and I try to make ours as happy a holiday-time home as I can.

Unfortunately, holidays are the biggest show night of the year. Everybody else wants to see you perform as part of their festivities. That makes family life for a performer especially difficult. For Velma, it became one more ob-struction in a marriage already strewn with roadblocks.

I did everything I could to keep things in balance, like a juggler with his pins, until, finally, I couldn't keep them all in the air at the same time. Everything in my life fell to the ground in one loud crash. The details aren't important but the results meant everything. Suffice it to say, life on the road, missing family get-togethers over the holidays, the realities of separation—none of this made for a happy marriage, for Velma or for me. After thirteen years to-gether of trying to make it work, we knew it was over and decided to end it. I sold the big house I had bought in Queens, and moved back to the old familiar terry in Au-gusta, Georgia, where I not only felt relieved, but at home.

Unlike when I had moved to New York, location was less important to me now. The reason was that I was mak-ing enough money to be able to add a second Learjet to my traveling itinerary, so even from Augusta, I could get to anywhere in the country I had to be, quickly and effi-ciently. New York City and the Apollo might have been the creative center of the music world, but Augusta was my home, and I was happy to be back.

While I was on tour in '66, I met the woman who was to become my next wife, Deidre Jenkins. Deedee, as I called her, was of mixed heritage, like I was, with some Jewish blood in her, which I liked because I've always admired the Judeo-Christian way of life. We first made each other's acquaintance while the band was playing one of those spots on the Maryland beaches. We started as friends but soon became intimate. We spoke early and often of marriage, but as my divorce from Velma was not yet finalized, we couldn't make the move. The truth was, at first I was in no hurry to get divorced, seeing that as long as I was still married to Velma, it might prevent me from making the same mistake again. But once I knew that Deedee and I were going to be together, I had my lawyers get to work on those papers.

Deedee was a wonderful woman, a good wife, and she proved to be a great mother, blessing me this time around with two beautiful daughters.

I bought a nice little home for us on Walton Way, which just happens to be one of the most exclusive White neighborhoods in Augusta. It's within eyesight, but that's all, of the ghetto. A lot of people asked me at the time why I wanted to live there, and I'd just smile and say, "I don't mind living next door to all those rich White folks. I'm not prejudiced!"

I was happy at home, but as always, being a husband and a daddy was not enough, and soon I had the itch to get back performing before live audiences. It was 1966. "Papa's Got a Brand New Bag" was still riding high on the charts. My touring schedule was heavier than it had ever been. And because of what was going on in the streets of an

America divided by the Vietnam War, I unavoidably became more aware of the politics, as much as the pop charts, of America. What Black man, or for that matter, any man, could not be outraged by what had happened to James Meredith on June 6, 1966, during his March Against Fear. Meredith, the first Black student admitted to the University of Mississippi back in 1962, was shot by a sniper during the march he himself organized.

Ironically, the March Against Fear proved an apt phrase. People were being intimidated, especially in the South, by the various Klans and what-have-you that were angered by the progress my people were making. And it wasn't just against Blacks that they were expressing their hatred. When those three unfortunate boys, Schwerner, Chaney, and Goodman—two White, one Black Freedom Fighters—had been killed in June 1964, one for being a "nigger" and two for being "nigger lovers," the entire country, Black and White, was disgusted, as the senseless brutality of the murders put the civil rights struggle in the forward conscience of every decent American.

When Mr. Meredith was gunned down during his march, I dropped everything to visit him in his hospital room in Mississippi. I was greatly affected by that visit, and afterward, I intensified the pledge I had made to myself that began with "Papa." It was no longer going to be enough to change the music of a generation—I had to try to change people's way of thinking as well. I wanted Black people to take more pride in who they were and to stand up against this rising tide of racism that was trying to drown us all.

This marked another, vital and fundamental change in the direction of my music, coming at a time when my popularity was at its peak. Make no mistake, I was warned once again by everyone I knew—friends, relatives, record people, everyone—not to do it. I was repeatedly told that if I just kept my cool, which I took to mean just continuing to do an acceptable, if hip, "buck-and-wing" and stay in my benign, soul-tinged, polite "Blackface," I would always be rich and famous and allowed to stay on Whitey's Easy Street for as long as I wanted. All I had to do, they said, was to continue to paint my world sunshine White.

No way, I told them. The time had come to paint it *real*. No matter what the price.

One of the first things I did was agree to perform for free at the June 6, 1966, concert to support the March Against Fear, an organized reaction to the Meredith shooting. I wanted to make a statement to the world at that show, through my music and my appearance, and I did. From now on there was going to be more Black pride in my music, meaning a more political element to my show, and to my being. Now that I had earned the right to be a cultural influence, I was going to put it to good use and apply it for the good of my people.

If there was an element of personal danger involved,

that was all right with me. I was a tough guy, I knew I could take the heat, and I knew my people knew it. If I didn't act or look scared, neither would they, I kept telling myself. Still, from that moment on, I never knew when I stepped on the stage if some maniac was waiting for me out there in the back with a rifle that held a bullet with my name on it. My songs began to reflect the images that were dominating the way I was thinking. In "Don't Be a Dropout:" *Tell me, everybody, one more time what I said. Without an education, you might as well be dead. . . .*

Whenever I wasn't onstage, I'd make time to talk to groups of young Black boys and girls, sometimes as few as a dozen or so, and I always gave them the same rap. Coming from me, I hoped it would mean something to them. If I saved even one of them from a wasted life, I considered it a total victory on my part. I'd always talk straight to them, and always pushed education. My rap went something like this: "I never had a chance to experience growing up as a kid. I was sixteen years old when I was taken by the authorities, the police. I was the most popular kid in the terry at the time, but really I was a bad kid and I had no self-esteem. Now don't you make the same mistake and be like I was, and start to think you're down below everybody else. You keep your head high and do what you gotta do . . . as a people."

I like to believe that message hit home. I had to think it

did, or there was no other way I could continue to be an entertainer in such a troubled time.

That's why it was especially important that I didn't come off as patronizing, or doing something for publicity, or just paying lip service to a cause. Too many people in show business like to get caught up in the beauty rather than in the power of their own words. I wanted to avoid all of that. I wanted to back up my talk with positive action. To do so, I created a series of scholarship funds for poor Black boys and girls, to make sure they could get a chance to go to school. I didn't make a big deal out of it at the time and I'm not trying to pat myself on the back now. To me, it was an absolute necessity, a battle against the racism that was coming to a head. I had made a lot of money, and knew that most of it had come out of the same ghettos where these kids who couldn't afford an ed-ucation lived. I wanted to—I *needed* to—give them some-thing back.

Nevertheless, none of this ever got a single mention in the press, and I couldn't understand why, especially when, if I ever crossed my eyes in public, it was an automatic headline. I guess it wasn't in the best interests of the es-tablishment press in those days (or these days either, for that matter) to hold me up as some kind of affirmative role model in the eyes of the people in my community. A rich, young, tough Black soul and funk performer who wanted to help kids stay on the good foot? I couldn't understand that. How much more difficult would it then be to publish stories about me as the drugged-out, wife-beating, lunatic Black guy who somehow got lucky and sold a few records? That stuff they could never get enough of.

I know that a lot of people who read this are going to think I'm trying to make excuses, for then and for more recent events, to rewrite history and current situations, to put a better image on myself in the eyes of the public. Well, I don't care if they do. I know, and my people know, that that simply isn't the case. I'm not saying I didn't do some things that were wrong, because I did. I can't undo it, and all I can say is, whatever happened happened. I didn't know any better. At the same time I did do some good things, like trying to use my influence to help those less fortunate than me, and I guess that just wasn't as good a story to a lot of people in the media. I did what I did for others, not to promote myself. I didn't need to—I was already there, at the head of my generation's multicultural class.

SEVEN

BIG-TIME CHANGE WAS A-COMIN' TO THE MAINSTREAM culture of America. There had been a time not too long ago when Black comedians could not even perform for White audiences. When they finally were allowed to, they could only do sketch comedy, usually playing the buffoon in one form or another. It took an awfully long time for the Black man to be able to simply come out on a stage, address the audience directly, and do a monologue for mixed audiences. Men like Richard Pryor were pioneers in this field. It was a hard-fought battle for all of us, but one we as Black entertainers eventually won.

I can remember when Flip Wilson was at his peak. His acceptance was based solely on the amiability of his humor. He was making breakthroughs, no question, but there was still a price on his head, so to speak, a purchasing of his talent to keep it in a certain acceptable place. A lot of that changed during the years the Reverend Dr. Martin Luther King Jr. rose to prominence, in the late fifties until his assassination in 1968. When the end came for him, there was such violence in the air because a lot of Black people felt they had had enough. Medgar Evers, Emmett Till, those three little girls in the church, the endless lynchings—all were the unmistakable signs of a national race war in which we were being wiped out systematically. Dr. King's murder looked to be the place where Black people were going to draw the line.

Ironically, the year 1968 had started on a personal high note for me. I had made enough money through my music to do something I'd always wanted to do: I bought my first radio station. This made all the sense in the world to me. If I was making music—the main product that the stations needed—and I would always have to rely on those stations to play it, then why not be the supplier as well as the recipient of my own product? One thing I knew was that this was one sure way my music would always get heard. I intended to build my own network, and the first step to that goal was the purchase of WGYW, in Knoxville, Tennessee. Once it was mine, I changed the call letters to WJBE.

It was a significant purchase for several reasons. First, as I mentioned before, it would guarantee an outlet for my own music, and the music of others I might produce and distribute. Second, the station had been silent for several months for financial reasons, and was therefore a missing Black voice in a Southern community where it was sorely needed. When I took it back on the air, I programmed soul, gospel, and jazz, with a little bit of talk here and there, and a lot of messages to the kids I knew would be listening to stay in school and get an education, the only weapon that would ever truly get them out of the ghetto. The station was a success, and soon I added several more, including WEBB in Baltimore and WRDW in Augusta, right in my own backyard.

Being connected in this new way to the media taught me a lot of things, mostly about the news of the world that I really hadn't paid all that much attention to in the past. The Vietnam War was raging, and all signs pointed to America becoming involved in something far worse and for much longer than we had originally thought. My immediate reaction was to go there. I always liked to be where the action was. I figured if Bob Hope could do it, why couldn't I?

I had my people get in touch with the USO, and to make sure there would be no unforeseen obstacles or delays, I volunteered to pay for everything—my own expenses, airfare, the cost of bringing my show over, everything.

Guess what? The USO said no.

Without explanation.

One big fat no.

But I wouldn't give up. I got together with Robert Johnson, the Black entrepreneur out of Chicago and the publisher of *Jet* magazine, and he helped me to convince the government that I should be allowed to make this trip. Eventually, Mr. Johnson was able to get me an audience with Vice President Hubert Humphrey, who in turn went directly to President Lyndon Johnson for an immediate approval. It wasn't that difficult to convince them that, in light of Mr. Johnson's troubles at the polls, it might not be so bad for the public to know that a Black man of some prominence, especially one who came up from the ghettos, actually wanted to go to Vietnam.

By now I was more than a little disgusted with the absurdity of it all. Before me, every major entertainer who went over to see the troops was White. It just didn't make any sense, and I'm sure it did nothing for the morale of the Black soldiers, who needed as much of a taste of home as their White brothers-in-arms. Understand, I didn't go to make anything even between Blacks and Whites, and I didn't want to entertain *only* Blacks. My goal was to entertain all the troops, regardless of their race. As far as I'm concerned, talent comes in any color and so do audiences. My music was intended for everybody. For God's army. And it bothered me that because I was Black I was being prevented from providing it.

I want to say one thing more here about Mr. Humphrey. It's funny with politicians. They may not always be as popular with the public, but on a one-to-one basis, they are almost always decent fellows, and Mr. Humphrey was a very decent man. Because he had agreed to meet with me, I made it my business to get to know him better. He struck me as a practical, smart man who understood the realities of life. He was far more of an independent politician than the public ever knew, because his image was that of a typical toe-the-line vice president.

Having still not received the green light to go to 'Nam, I went to see him several more times. At this time I was also having a tax problem and wondered if he might be able to help me, or at least give me advice as to where to look for help. He listened to me patiently, shook his head every now and then, and when I was finished, took a deep breath and said, "Mr. Brown, there's no room in America for independence anymore."

I asked him where that came from, and he said, "If there had been, I'd be president today." It was an interesting comment about how the system works, and the limitations of what one can do within it. I understood what he was saying to me, and I never raised that issue or any other having to do with me personally again. For the rest of my visit that day, we talked about the notion of independence, the meaning of it, and what the value was of belonging to a party in power. It was fascinating and enlightening to me, particularly when he talked about the price one pays for freedom in the real world.

The next time we met, I was still trying to get to Vietnam and was still running into that same political brick wall. He knew what the situation was and said that he understood why I was having trouble. He knew that there was always a worry that a Black man might have an agenda for the Black soldiers that wasn't exactly what the powers that be wanted. And he was sharp enough to know that that wasn't what James Brown was all about. Again he promised to do everything he could to help me.

You may not believe this, or may not want to, but at one point he talked to me about the idea of my being his running mate if he ran again for president! Of course the idea didn't go very far, but I have to admit it was intriguing. If something like that ever happened and by some miracle I was elected, I would have tried to change certain things in America while always being careful not to upset the apple-cart of democracy. For sure I'd have put the whole country in a brand-new bag.

I knew that some people, Blacks as much as Whites, didn't like my association with Mr. Humphrey. Black people thought he was not working hard enough to bring justice to the Black man in America, but as I got to know him, I realized how wrong that assumption was. Like so many politicians, they are far different from how the media makes them out to be.

Take Governor Lester Maddox. He was one of the most reviled men in the Black community for all the racist damage he had done and for the racists remarks he had said about Southern Black men. However, once he convinced the White men in his state he didn't like Blacks and was given all the power, among the first things he did was to release unjustly jailed Blacks from prison. I got to know Governor Maddox quite well. He became one of my closest friends, and one of the best friends Southern Blacks ever had. I'd like to think that our getting to know each other was as much a revelation for him as it was for me.

Governor George Wallace was the same thing. He started off full of anger and hate for the Black man. Remember the "Segregation before, segregation now, segregation forever!" speech he made? He, too, became another of my best friends. He used to call me Brother Brown, and that always put a huge smile on my face. One day toward the end of his life, he took me aside and said, "Brother Brown, if I had known the things I know now about Black people, I would never have said all the bad things about them that I did." He came to understand the simplest and most profound meaning of brotherhood—I'm not going to tell you I'm better than you, and I don't want you to tell me that you're better than me.

Interestingly, a Black man by the name of Floyd, who was a good friend of mine until he died, wheeled Governor Wallace around during the last years of his life. They knew and loved each other quite a lot. I always thought the governor was shot and paralyzed because he had a real chance of winning the presidential election in 1972. Because he didn't belong to either of the two parties, he posed a real threat to the status quo of race relations in America, particularly in the Old South.

You see, people can learn, and people can change, and that is why I always approached life with a smile and a polite manner, to lead by example rather than by anger and violence. One always worked for us as a people; the other never did for anybody.

Still, by now I was getting more angry and frustrated about being prevented from going to Vietnam, and began to formulate the next stage of my attack when suddenly word came to me that Mr. Syd Nathan had died. It was a terrible blow. Yes, we had had our differences both personally and creatively, and there were those numerous lawsuits between us. Money had kind of gotten in our way, but still, he had been there at the beginning, had helped to start my career off, and had always given me my head in the recording studio, even if I had to pay for that privilege. I loved him and he loved me and he was as responsible as anybody for bringing James Brown to the world.

The death of Mr. Nathan was a major loss, but it would not be the last in this pivotal year, for James Brown and for the country.

The next to go was Little Willie John. This was the year he died in prison, never getting to see free daylight again. Then, that March, just as I was starting a four-day stint at the Apollo, word came to me that the great tap dancer Honi Coles was gone. Mr. Coles and I had become close during the many times we had shared the Apollo stage. The shows I did the rest of that year were especially emotional, my personal tribute to Mr. Nathan, Little Willie, and Mr. Coles.

I also continued my charitable work, and one night onstage I donated a fairly hefty check to the president of the Congress of Racial Equality (CORE), and one to the H. Rap Brown Defense Fund as well. I wasn't particularly fond of Student Nonviolent Coordinating Committee (SNCC) but I was adamant about Mr. Brown's right to say what he wanted, and to act with all the authority granted to him in the Constitution. In other words, as with so many other leaders, I may not have completely agreed with what he had to say—all that "burn baby burn" stuff—but I was willing to put my money where my mouth was to defend to the death his right to say it.

That April, I boarded a plane and headed for Africa, to visit the Ivory Coast. It was to be my first trip to the homeland, and I was excited about it. Funny enough, when we landed, I felt as if I were returning somewhere rather than stepping onto the soil of a land I'd never been to before. It's called heritage, I guess.

Nevertheless, Africa was the strangest place I had ever seen in my life. I passed through Dar es Salaam on my way to Nigeria and sensed this unusual spirituality in the air. Interestingly, the more time I spent there, the more I felt that

I understood my people better than I ever had before. Meanwhile, I was offered a fortune to play Sun City, in South Africa. I probably would have done it at another time in my life, but I had become so aware of apartheid and all the troubles there that I simply said no. I was told a lot of others had gone there and "gotten away with it," but that didn't move me one bit. Nor did the $3 million they dangled in front of me *for two performances in two days*. I said no and I meant no, and that decision stood. I did not take the offer, because I did not believe in working for blood money.

As for the rest of Africa, I was overwhelmed by the fact that I'd see kids walking around in the streets, wherever I went, with James Brown albums under their arms—four, five, six different ones. And what truly made that amazing was they didn't have phonographs to play them on. They just wanted to have the records with them. I found out that one of my albums cost those kids more money than they made in a whole year. What they would do is go into town and use a communal phonograph whenever they wanted to hear them. I admired that spirit and determination, and it told me something about these kids. One day they were going to run the country, and when they did, they would see to it that some changes were made. This was a generation that was told what they *better* do for the good of the government, and they responded with what they *had* to do, for the good of themselves.

And change the country they did!

I would have preferred to remain in Africa for months—
years, even—as I felt the strong pull of my ancestors. This
was far different from reading about history—this was
walking in it. Here I was, in a land where Black meant
something other than "Hey, you" or "You're not welcome
here." Leaving America for this trip, I found a new sense of
who I was, where I had come from, and where I wanted to
go. Like other prominent American Blacks, including
Muhammad Ali, Malcolm X, and Richard Pryor, my visit to
Africa was a profound experience for me, life-affirming and
life-changing. I had no idea how much and how quickly
those changes were about to take place.

I stayed in Africa for only five days before returning to
the States because of my touring obligations. I had booked
a huge spring show at the Boston Garden, which had sold
out immediately. The show was scheduled for a Friday
night, and I intended to go through with it, even though
the day before the most shattering news imaginable (or
unimaginable) came to me via the deep-voiced bulletins
over the radio: *The Reverend Dr. Martin Luther King has
been murdered today by a sniper's bullet in Memphis, Tennessee, while standing on the balcony of his motel room!*

I was devastated. I didn't know what to do, and even
though I had to do my show, I wondered what would happen in the aftermath of such a national tragedy. That
Thursday, the day after the assassination, Mayor Kevin
White of Boston urged me to put the concert on television

so that anyone who wanted to could see it. His reason was a simple and obvious one: that Friday night, with no school the next day, everyone in Boston was gritting their teeth, getting ready for the street riots that were sure to come. There was a rumbling of fury in the air that would not go away.

The local soul station, WILD, led by a disk jockey named Early Byrd, helped set the broadcast up, and soon had gotten WGBH, the local outlet of the public television system, to agree to broadcast the show live.

What nobody counted on was the effect the announcement had on the ticket buyers. There was bad air already, and anyone in his right mind—especially if he were White—would not want to venture out onto Boston's mean streets to see a Black show, especially if it was going to be on TV for free. Even though I was going to take a financial bath, I knew I had to go on and do my thing to keep the peace. There are some things more important than money.

The show began with Mayor White saying a few opening words, the most important of which were: "We in Boston shall honor Dr. Martin Luther King in peace." He was more or less pleading with the almost exclusively Black audience to honor the memory of Dr. King with a nonviolent evening of music. He then introduced Thomas Atkins, the first Black city councilman in the history of Boston, who in turn introduced me. As the lights dimmed and the focus of the spotlight sharpened, I came out from behind the curtain, just as it began to part.

Before I started singing, I spoke directly to the audience in the house, and everyone at home watching. "Let's not do anything to dishonor Dr. King," I said. Then I looked directly into one of the big cameras there onstage. "You kids, especially, I want you to stay home tonight and think about what Dr. King stood for. Don't just react in a way that's going to destroy your community."

Having said my piece, I began the show.

Everything went well, until the finale, when some of the kids rushed onto the stage, and the police, thinking this was the beginning of the riot, overreacted and literally began to push and throw them off the stage. I didn't know what else to do, so I kept on singing. In response, a lot of the kids started dancing and singing with me, and that really annoyed the police.

Then, without warning, one of the uniforms came charging toward a little kid standing right next to me who was just kind of strutting his stuff and trying to feel good dancing with James Brown. I looked directly at the officer, put my hands up, and said, "It's all right. . . . I'm all right. I'm all right," and asked him to please back off. "I *want* to shake their hands," I said, and began shaking every hand in sight. After a few minutes of letting these youngsters have their moment in the spotlight, I asked them as nicely as I could to go back to their seats. Some of them did, some of them didn't. I went to the mike and, with my cape around my shoulders, started talking to what was turning into an increasingly unruly mob.

"Ah, look, wait a minute, wait a minute. . . . Let me finish the show up, all right? Now step down. . . ." When they didn't, I continued, knowing that I had to get control over the situation, and fast. It was all going to come down to respect; that was the message I knew I had to get across. Respect for me, respect for themselves.

"You makin' me look bad. . . . I asked you to step down and you wouldn't and that's wrong. . . . You're not being fair to yourselves and me neither . . . or your race. . . . Now I asked the authorities to step back because I thought that I could get some respect from my own people."

With that, they finally started to calm down and I knew I was going to be all right. "Now are we together or ain't we?" A cheer went up, I turned to the band, counted them down to "I Can't Stand It," and I was back in business.

People still ask me if I was frightened that night, and of course the answer is, I wasn't. I was with those kids every step of the way, and knew that they would not do anything they shouldn't. They wanted an explanation, a reason why, not more violence. I believed in them, and because of it, I sang my heart out until two in the morning, without a lick of trouble in the Garden or anywhere in the streets of Boston. I'm told it was so quiet that night it was like a ghost town, as it was in any of the number of cities that had decided at the last minute to carry the broadcast.

I thought that was going to be the end of it, until the next morning when word came to me that Washington, D.C., was literally on fire. I was stunned. I turned on the TV and saw our national capital in flames. I was asked to go down there and speak to the people, and of course, I agreed. Once I arrived, just before I went in front of a crowd of shouting Black people, the authorities asked me what I was going to say, sounding a bit worried. Maybe I was going to pour a little gasoline on those spouting flames. I told them that I wasn't going to say anything that the people didn't understand. That didn't seem to do it for them, and they asked me if I had any notes they could see. I said no, I didn't. Not to worry, I told them. I live with these people every day. I'll say and do what's right for you, what's right for me, and what's right for them.

Clearly, only someone who had earned a measure of respect from the community was going to be able get through this situation. It was difficult, I think, for the White authorities to understand the outrage that Dr. King's murder had sparked in the Black community. This was a man they dearly loved, who died for something he shouldn't even have had to be fighting for in the first place.

Finally, I went before the crowd, and in a speech that was televised live from the Municipal Center, I implored the people to *think*—to think about Dr. King's message, and to give their actions a second thought before they continued on the path they had chosen. Although most in attendance were Black, I felt I wasn't speaking to any one color or race, but to *humanity*. I was trying to make a difference because of who I was, and who I had become in the world of entertainment.

The riots stopped, and order slowly returned to the streets. That made me feel really good. In my own small way, I knew that I had prevented a lot of damage from being done, and maybe even some deaths.

Unfortunately, my good feelings were not contagious, especially with the authorities. There was a lot of suspicion, especially among the national police, the FBI, and the CIA about this so-called display of "Black Power" on my part. Their thinking went something along the lines of, if he could stop a riot that easily (although how they came to think what had happened that night was "easy" I'll never know), he could just as easily start one. From that moment I knew I was put under national security surveillance. I felt like there were government eyes everywhere, because there were. Somehow, they were able to see me through TV, using some kind of special reverse X-rays or something. I ran out and bought sunglasses to protect my eyes and my brain while I watched. I felt a little like I was in that movie with Sharon Stone, *Sliver*, where everyone was under some kind of TV surveillance, even in the privacy of their own homes. Of course with me, it wasn't some crazy killer in a movie doing it—it was real life, and it was the government. I could sense them watching me, spying on me, staking out my home.

All of that notwithstanding, I did what I did because it was my patriotic duty to do so, out of love for my country and the desire to see my people safe and secure during those terrible times immediately following the assassination of Dr. King. As far as I could tell, the Black pride that mushroomed in the sixties helped to propel the civil rights movement forward. And despite all the setbacks, murders, and violence, it is the same pride I feel today, the same pride we need today, maybe even more than ever, a social, cultural, and economic stepping-stone to a better tomorrow.

EIGHT

IT WAS ONLY A FEW WEEKS AFTER DR. KING'S ASSASSI-
nation when I was finally given the official clearance to
go to Vietnam, and within days I found myself in the
heat of the battle. I knew that our Black brothers and sisters were hungry for some entertainment that they could
identify with more readily than what they were getting.
However, much to my surprise, even with all the official
interference blocking my trip behind me, my decision
proved not all that popular in the Black community. Right
up until the time I left for 'Nam I continued to receive
stern warnings from certain Black leaders that by going
over there I was, in effect, supporting an extremely unpopular war, and because of it, I was hurting not just myself
but my people.

What made things even worse, for them, was that I had accepted a personal invitation from President Lyndon Johnson to dine with him at the White House, his way of saying thanks for my support. My acceptance was taken as an insult by many in the Black community who did not support Mr. Johnson, even though in 1964, one of the first things LBJ did as president was to sign into law the most important civil rights act of modern times. And despite the fact that I was willing to give up a hundred thousand dollars' worth of private earnings from shows I had to cancel to make the trip, I was still seen as some kind of "sellout."

The dinner with LBJ at the White House took place even as the government brass and the USO were ironing out the final terms—limitations really—under which I could actually go to Vietnam. The one that bothered me the most was that they wanted us all to carry weapons. I questioned that. We were going there to entertain, not to kill anyone. Did Bob Hope carry a gun?

Well, they said, what if you're attacked?

Okay, so we're attacked. That's why we have soldiers there, to protect us. *Soldiers who know what they're doing.*

I arrived in Vietnam at the end of May 1968. We first flew to South Korea, and there began to do our series of shows for the servicemen. The core group I was able to take along included superb musicians as well as very brave men. Sadly, with the exception of Danny Ray, my so-called "Cape Man," they've all passed on. There were

Waymon Reed on guitar, Clyde Shubble on drums, and Tim Drummond on bass. I loved them all dearly, and take my hat off to them for the contribution they made to entertain our boys. Tim Drummond volunteered to go because he felt that soldiers seeing a White man and a Black man sharing the stage together was a good thing, and I agreed. We weren't there just to entertain Black troops; we were there to entertain all the servicemen who were in Vietnam, no matter what their color. We were about music and support, not politics and race.

Things got worse when *Life* magazine put my picture on the cover with this question alongside it, in big, nervous headlines: "Is This the Most Important Black Man in America?" I was being treated with mockery by the White mainstream media and at the same time branded by Blacks as an Uncle Tom. It was the kind of broad-based criticism I was to be subjected to for the rest of my career. No matter what I did, the event connected to my name would become less important than the question of my own motivation, ethics, and character. I have learned that patriotism and being free sometimes come at a hefty price when you're Black and famous.

Earl Wilson, who was a very influential syndicated newspaper columnist in the sixties, and White, intensified the public's feelings and said outright what had previously only been hinted at, when he asked me, on the record, if I didn't think that by dining with LBJ and going to Vietnam I was some kind of Uncle Tom. Although I bristled at the question, I remained cool and tried to explain to him what my true motivations were. "No," I told him, "I'm not an Uncle Tom. No one who serves his president and entertains his country's troops can be an Uncle Tom. Unless a man is willing to fight for his country he has nothing else to fight for, and those men deserve to know we are thinking of them back home, and supporting them. I'm an American all the way through to my soul." After that, Mr. Wilson became one of the few journalists not afraid to back me up in print, and I think it helped my standing somewhat in the Black community.

Still, the conflicted feelings among Americans weren't hard to miss, and choosing to align myself with a president increasingly sympathetic to Blacks and voluntarily traveling to a highly unpopular war only kept me in the eye of the cultural hurricane that was brewing throughout the United States. Poor Black kids all over America were becoming increasingly angry about being drafted to fight in a war for the freedom of the Vietnamese people, a freedom they knew they didn't fully enjoy at home.

The great Muhammad Ali had refused to be inducted to fight against non-White people and because of it the government took away his license to box and tried to throw him in prison. He insisted that it was against his religion to fight and that he only wanted what we all wanted—the real freedom for his people to get a fair chance to make it in America.

And here I was, fighting against a tremendous amount of resistance to be allowed to go to Vietnam!

I didn't care. I thought it was important to make a statement via the same media that was spreading so many inaccurate messages about me and about my people. According to the newspapers and TV networks, no Black people wanted to go to Vietnam to defend their country. That simply wasn't the case. There were many Blacks who did their patriotic duty without complaint. I thought it was a good thing to lead by example and show that I was willing, eager even, to do my thing for the soldiers. Black kids needed to know that we hadn't forgotten about them, that we cared about them, and that they deserved as much entertainment and support as the White kids were getting from Bob Hope.

Please don't misunderstand; to me, Bob Hope was one of the greatest Americans who ever lived. What's more, and a lot of people don't know this, he helped make my trip finally happen by using his personal and considerable influence within the USO to grease some crucial wheels and get me going. I appreciated his help, although the entire time I was over there the USO kept close tabs on my entire entourage, and because of this, it made the trip far more difficult and dangerous for us than it ever had to be. They severely limited the number of musicians I could bring with me, which made no sense as the whole purpose of my going was to entertain. Nor was I there to fight the enemy. I was simply there to comfort our own soldiers, but you never would have known it from the rather distant, condescending fashion in which I was treated the whole time by the official brass.

Let me tell you one of the most extraordinary moments that took place during our trip. It happened at a base, while we were doing our thing, and playing the music as loud as possible. Suddenly, all the shooting that was always going on in the background, just over the hills it seemed, stopped. Everyone knew what was going on. The other side was enjoying our music just as much as our own boys. In effect, the James Brown Revue had brought a temporary cease-fire to the war! If only we could have expanded that and ended the whole thing with one gigantic, mutual, bilateral chorus of "I Feel Good."

We traveled around the countryside a lot, doing two, sometimes three shows a day, heading out from Saigon every evening into the countryside by helicopter, which, as I was to find out, was more than a little dangerous because of the pervasive presence of the enemy and their ground-to-air weaponry. One time we came *this close* to getting popped! Several times we had to hit the deck of the helicopter, or the transport if it was a longer flight, while bullets whizzed by, sometimes inches from our heads, meant to kill us. I mean, it was intense. At one point during a show we came under attack. There were men in uniform all over the place, weapons being fired, and again I could hear the lead buzz by my head. Fortunately, I wasn't there long enough to understand how dangerous this all was, or to have any real idea of what we were actually facing. In truth, while the USO and the government were so busy trying to prevent us from going, they had forgotten to show us what to do in the event of an attack. My only real training for these encounters came from, of all places, the war movies I had watched as a kid.

At one point we were on a stage when yet another attack took place. Charlie came through, sprayed the area with bullets, and as soon as the smoke cleared, I got up, grabbed a mike, and resumed singing. As always, music proved to be my and everyone else's salvation. This time, when the spotlight came back on me, even as the gunfire continued, I looked up and let the words of a different song from the one I had been singing come spilling out of my mouth: *My country 'tis of thee, sweet land of liberty . . . of thee I sing. . . .* It was an amazing moment, filled with drama, irony, patriotism, and privilege. I suddenly felt closer to God than I ever had before.

It also crossed my mind that maybe carrying weapons hadn't been such a bad idea after all.

Another time we were in a helicopter, and it was actually hit. Fortunately, we were able to land, another helicopter came and picked us up, and we were off once more, as if nothing had happened. It was a bit too unbelievable! Now, for the first time, I understood why so many of the soldiers

were taking drugs, and doing all kinds of things they normally wouldn't do. They were, after all, facing death every
day, and whatever got them through it was okay, because it
was their lives that were on the line. They never knew when
it was going to be their turn; most of them were just kids
who had not really begun to live their lives. If I had to face
that kind of situation, you'd better believe I'd take any kind
of drug available. Nothing would be out of bounds in my
fight to survive. That's the common knowledge of the
street, and most of the boys who were in the combat zones
were street kids who knew how to fight and how to survive.

Still, a lot of them caught it, and I made it a point to
visit as many wounded soldiers in their temporary hospi-
tals as I could. I saw men with no legs, no arms, missing
faces, soldiers lying there in tubed-up agony.

Although I was only in Vietnam for a brief time, I felt as
if I now understood the world in a way I hadn't before. Being on the front lines had made me aware of just how endless the fight against racism really was. I saw White men
and Black men fighting Yellow men. And it depressed and
saddened me.

Upon touching down on American soil again, I felt the
only way to shake this depression over our sorry state of
affairs was to do the one thing I knew how to do—to get
away from the reality of war, I sought the peace of music.

Shortly after my return I began to work on a new song,
and by August 1968 it was ready for release. The title was

"Say It Loud, I'm Black and I'm Proud." It was an entirely different kind of song for me, heavily influenced as it was by the murder of Dr. King and my trip to Vietnam. I was eager to record a song with a message of pride aimed directly at my own people, a reminder that standing up with pride was the best way to combat any and all assaults against us, be it murder in Memphis or the defense of liberty in Vietnam. I know a lot of people, both White and Black, had never heard anything like it before, not just from me, but from *any* performer. This was not going to be just another hit record by a Black entertainer like my dear friend Sammy Davis Jr.'s "Candy Man." This was *the real thing*, a wake-up call, a rallying cry, a statement of *pride*.

I recorded it in Hollywood, and I wanted it to sound as if there were a million people singing along with me in the studio. I asked everyone who was involved with the recording to bring their friends, their relatives, anybody they knew. They didn't have to be able to sing to be a part of this composition.

I'll tell you a little story about the recording of "Say It Loud." A few weeks before I cut it, just after I had returned from Vietnam, I had met again with the Democratic presidential candidate Hubert Humphrey. Mr. Humphrey was now running for president, and while not inviting me onto the ticket (what chance, really, did that have?), he asked me to campaign for him in Watts, the infamous hotbed of riots in California. It was a difficult decision for me, as privately I had supported Bobby Kennedy, and had been badly shaken by his assassination, coming as it did only months after Dr. King had been killed. I gave it a lot of thought, and I decided I would get up on the platform with Mr. Humphrey, and see if I couldn't get him to commit to a few things he so far hadn't.

To my surprise, Mr. Humphrey was loudly booed at every event we attended. Surrounded by dozens of bodyguards, he didn't exactly look like a leader to me. Instead he seemed scared and indecisive. I took this as my cue to publicly confront him about the issues that were important to me. One time he surprised me during an appearance and asked me publicly for my official endorsement. I turned to him on the platform we were sharing and said I certainly would endorse him, if he promised then and there to help Black people in America get a step up in business, gain the opportunity to build and own their own motels, restaurants, retail establishments, auto dealerships—all the things that we had been denied for so long because of our color.

I remember how he looked at me kind of funny, as if he had no idea what I was talking about. No wonder, I thought to myself, he was being booed. After waiting a beat, he went to the microphone and said that if he were elected president, he would get all those things for us. Now the crowd cheered. I said okay, then, I'll endorse you. The music played, we both danced, and I came away with the feeling that somehow I had been able to make a difference, that I had gotten someone who might become the next president of the United States to at least make a promise to my people that was on the record.

I was still feeling pretty good about it the night of the recording session for "Say It Loud." Just before I left for the studio, I could hear something in the hallway outside of my hotel room. I opened the door and there, on the floor, where the room service trays were usually placed at the end of a meal, was a bomb.

I could tell immediately it wasn't real. I knew enough about street explosives to see that right away. But it could have been, and it might as well have been, for the surge of fear that it sent through me. No one was safe in this world, I thought to myself at that moment, not even *me*. But I didn't stay scared. I closed the door, went back into my room, got dressed, and kept telling myself over and over again, "I'm Black and I'm *proud*. . . . I'm Black and I'm *proud*. . . ."

Unfortunately, while the song was a clear message to Black people, the White community took it entirely the wrong way, as a kind of aggressive statement meant to induce fear. They found it hostile and provocative, and used it as proof that even though I had endorsed a moderate for president, I had turned militant. Of course I hadn't at all. Just the opposite was true. The song was meant as my rallying cry for peaceful self-pride.

Things weren't helped by the fact that many of the more militant Black organizations in the country, most notably

SNCC and the Black Panthers, took my singsongy tune and turned it into their personal anthem, all but obliterating its peaceful and positive message. Still, at the time, I wondered—as I do today—would it have been seen as such a militant song if it had been called "I'm Irish and I'm Proud"? Or "I'm Italian and I'm Proud"? Or "I'm Jewish and I'm Proud"? Was it the song, or was it the race of the man who wrote it that had gotten people so angry?

Nevertheless, I paid the price for "Say It Loud." Even though it was a hit, it cost me a considerable part of my White audience that had so loyally supported my career by buying my records and coming to see my shows, two key factors that had helped deliver me into the mainstream of popular culture. So negative was the reaction to the song that radio programmers refused to play it on White stations.

It seemed that upon my return from Vietnam, everything I had worked for all my life began collapsing around me. Before I knew it my bookings fell off, and I quickly became something of a nonperson in pop music. I found myself back where I had started so long ago, playing in small clubs to predominantly Black faces, preaching to the choir, as it were. I told myself it didn't matter, that I was Black, that I was proud, that I was trying to tell the world how much better I thought things were going to be. And, I told myself, this was as bad as it could possibly get.

It wasn't.

Not long after the release of "Say It Loud," I began to have serious business problems. It started with the FCC. One of the radio stations I owned in Baltimore was having signal problems. The commission insisted it was because the station wasn't being properly maintained. There might have been some truth in that. I had given one of my sons the job of running it, and without a lot of experience, he was in a little bit over his head. Running a radio station is a very difficult thing to do. If you don't maintain your equipment, the signal you send out can drift and interfere with other stations, which, the FCC said, was happening. I asked them what they wanted me to do about it, expecting them to recommend a technical expert to fix the situation. Their actual answer amazed me. Sell out, they demanded, or we will take the station away from you.

I didn't know what to do. I tried to fight their ruling. I even asked my good friend Mr. Humphrey, who in the interim had lost the election to Richard Nixon, to help me out. I went to see him to remind him of his promise to help get more Black people their own businesses, not to see the government take them away. He gritted his teeth and told me there was nothing he could do. I thanked him and left.

While I still had others, it tore the heart out of me to have that particular station taken away. I remember the day I signed the papers to sell it—I had tears in my eyes.

With this forced sale, I knew a significant voice of the Black community was being lost. And so did the FCC, although I'm sure we had different reactions to that reality.

My bad run of misfortune didn't stop there. Even after I sold every last station and had promised myself that I would have nothing more to do with the business of radio, I somehow was dragged into the new round of payola scandals that emerged in the late sixties and early seventies. This was nothing new to me, and not even worth the paper the charges were printed on. Hell, payola had been a way of life in the music business since the beginning, and everyone participated in one form or another. Sure, the scandals of the late fifties were far more complex and involved issues that really had little to do with the business of rock and roll. This time, however, there was more than a hint that once again the government was using payola to silence yet another prominent Black figure in the industry, namely me—James Brown. I'm sure Dick Clark had no knowledge of it, but I used to pay *someone* in the chain a thousand dollars to get me on *American Bandstand.* Every time.

So what? What's wrong with a man selling his wares by taking a buyer to dinner? That's really all that my payola ever amounted to: spending money to make money, like every other business. For all the moral nonsense overlaid on it, the music business is just that—a business, and it is operated as all businesses are: with and for M-O-N-E-Y.

I was always a good target for some young government hotshot to try to make his reputation, like the punk gunslinger who shoots Gregory Peck in *The Gunfighter* so he can be the next big man. I have never hidden my feelings about how I ran my career and my business. Whenever I did a show, I hired a local DJ to emcee, and paid him for his work. Was that payola? I always paid their appearance fees, sometimes out of my own pocket when there wasn't enough advertising to cover the show's local costs. Was that payola, too? I paid my DJs in cash, but always got receipts from them, because I felt it was a legitimate business expense, the cost of doing business, as they say in the accounting schools. As long as the DJs got onstage, introduced me, and played a record of mine on their shows, I was satisfied. I wanted someone to do something for me, so I figured the best way was to do something for them. If they couldn't afford a new car, we'd get one for them, if we could afford it. Sometimes at Christmastime, I'd send over TV sets for everyone at the radio stations that played my records. What about that? Should I have been sent to the chair for such a heinous crime?

As far as I was concerned, business favors were the simple generosity of a man who was flush helping out a brother. I didn't see and still don't see anything wrong with it. It is simply the way business is done, as usual, in America, between White people every day of the week.

Still, no matter how rigorously we defended what we

did just to get our records played on the radio, my manager, Mr. Charles Bobbit, who had been handling my affairs since the first time I soloed at the Apollo, came very close to going to jail after admitting that we had paid Frankie Crocker, a famous New York–based disk jockey, for emceeing a couple of my appearances, after which he played our records on his radio show. I couldn't believe it! Was James Brown not famous enough to have his music heard anyway? Thankfully, Mr. Bobbit escaped going to jail on a technicality. Unfortunately, after that, if we weren't already poison to the White side of the industry, we surely were then.

In the late sixties I had a Hawker-Sidley private jet that I used to get to my shows; I had an agreement with Polydor, the new label I had signed with, to maintain it. After the payola scandal, they were afraid it might be construed as something illegal and refused to keep doing so. As a result I lost the plane. The day it was repossessed I said to myself, Well, brother, you know what? This is a good thing. You have gone too high in the sky! You are too far removed from the reality of your music and your people. Maybe, I told myself, I needed this to happen to remind me of who I am and what my real message still is. And yet there was a side of me that said, Why *couldn't* I own my own plane? Why shouldn't I be able to do and have everything the successful White man does? Did anyone object to Elvis flying around in *his* private plane?

NINE

I N 1971 I TOURED AFRICA AND EUROPE, WHERE I KNEW
my business problems in America would have no meaning to my devoted world fans. Thankfully, all they cared
about is my music. Sure enough, I sold out everywhere, including three straight nights at the world-famous Wembley
Stadium in London, England, and a few days later, I did
my thing before four hundred thousand eager fans in
Leeds. Word of this tour's astounding success made its way
back to the States, and even before I returned, I was offered a shot at what was then the hottest club in New York
City, and therefore the country: Jules Podell's legendary
Copacabana, right in the heart of midtown Manhattan.

Make that *White* midtown Manhattan, as Harlem
doesn't begin until several miles north, on the far side of

Central Park, where all the Black performers usually played when they said they were doing a gig in New York. South of Central Park, clubs were almost exclusively White, both in terms of the audiences and the performers. Yes, Sammy Davis Jr. occasionally played the Copa, but even he was forced by management to tone down his act—to cool down some of his heat—for the high-ticket White audiences. As a result he always wore a tuxedo, spoke in that funny faux-British accent that he occasionally used, sang mostly ballads, tap-danced a little, and as expected, knocked the place out. Even a laid-back Sammy could do it all: sing, dance, tell jokes, do impersonations, and work his rear end off to please the crowd.

Of course, what worked for him wasn't going to work for me. I did one thing—performed soul music. I sang it, I danced it, I went up on my toes and down to my knees with it. However, if I did the same kind of high-energy show for the two hundred people in the Copa's small room that I did for the two hundred thousand people at Wembley, there would be a nuclear crater on Forty-ninth Street and Broadway.

So I tried it the Copa way—that is to say, Mr. Podell's way—for the first of my scheduled two weeks at the famed club. Almost from the moment I took the stage, I knew something was wrong. The audiences weren't digging me, and I surely wasn't digging them. I was getting twenty-five thousand dollars a week, guaranteed, for two weeks—super money in those days. Very few Black rock and pop performers were getting anything like it in smaller venues: not Little Richard, not Chuck Berry, not even most White acts except Elvis Presley, and he hardly played anywhere anymore. The Copa was considered the top of the heap, the class among the class clubs, and the standard rule was that if Mr. Podell called upon you, you were supposed to consider yourself blessed, show up, and do exactly as you were told.

Now this Mr. Podell had a tough guy's demeanor. He didn't take any garbage from anybody, no matter how big and bad they were, or thought they were. His reputation preceded him like a pair of brass knuckles on a fist. But hey, you know what? I didn't care who he was or was supposed to be. I only had one boss when I hit the stage and that was me. If anybody thought they could do my act better than I could, they were welcome to try, including Mr. Podell.

By the end of the first week I had already made up my mind that I wasn't coming back for the second, not for twenty-five thousand dollars, not for twenty-five *million*. I wasn't going to tone down my show for *nobody*, because that would mean toning down *who I was*. The whole point of doing the show, the essence of the meaning of James Brown, was to be *myself*.

Mr. Podell was surprised by my decision, but I acted like a gentleman about it and so did he, and without making a big deal, he let me go. He seemed to not only understand, but agree with me that I would be better off, and so would the club, if I split.

The failure of my gig at the Copa confirmed for me what I had sensed was coming for a long time now. The times were rapidly changing, and so was I. What had begun twenty years earlier as an attempt at having a career in the small clubs on the Chitlin Circuit down south, beyond whose borders I was virtually unknown, had now taken me to the far corners of the world. Upon my return from Europe this time, I no longer felt at home among my American fans. It was obvious to me that they had changed—they were listening to new and different types of music. The war, civil rights, and the rise of the drug culture had affected the sensibilities of a generation. And I was no longer that naive young boy content to play small venues for a handful of people. As much as my audience had changed, so had I.

Perhaps the most obvious change came out of necessity. I had been looking for a new label for a while, and the death of Mr. Nathan coinciding with the end of my obligation to King Records made that search my top priority. When he passed, his partner, Hal Neely, bought out what was left of the company and renamed it Starday-King. A year later Neely sold it to Linn Broadcasting, based out of Nashville. I signed up with Mr. Neely, but soon became disenchanted with the Linn organization, mainly because they wouldn't play James Brown records on their own radio stations.

My attorney, Mr. Jack Pearl, then told me about a British

record company by the name of Polydor that was looking to expand into America, and asked me to consider signing on with them as distributors. Polydor already had distribution networks in England and Germany as part of a worldwide company known as N. V. Philips out of Holland and Siemens A.G. of West Germany (which is today one of the largest electronics equipment manufacturers in the world). I flat out refused. I vowed to never again sign a long-term contract with any record company, especially a foreign-based one. I had learned some hard lessons, probably the most important one being that you can't work for the Man in a business run by children. There was only one man I felt comfortable working for, and his name was James Brown. I had ideas of starting my own label and rediscovering myself.

At the same time, I met two brothers by the name of Julian and Roy Rifkin, who wined and dined and promised me the world if I would let them take over the management side of my business. I liked them a lot, and before I knew it, I signed a management deal with them, not knowing that they had done business with Polydor. Moreover, I found out that King Records was distributed internationally by Polydor. Everywhere I turned, it seemed I was already connected to what I was trying to get away from.

I began to get the creepy feeling that I couldn't escape the chains I was wearing, even if they were twenty-four-karat ones, like those that hung from the wrists of the Rifkins. As soon as I signed, they wasted no time acquiring Mercury

Records, a label I had actually been with for a brief time during the period I had left King Records. They also acquired all the rights to the music I had done for that label. Now they also wanted to buy Chri-Ted, my newly formed publishing company that controlled my post-King catalog, which I had named after two of my sons. But I wisely refused to sell it.

My first album for Polydor was *Hot Pants,* and we were off.

Unfortunately, we didn't go anywhere. Two or three albums later, it became clear to me that working with this new team, I just couldn't re-create the King label magic. That doesn't mean that I didn't make some exceptionally good records for Polydor, including "Make It Funky," "Get on the Good Foot," and "Get Up offa That Thing." I've never been quite sure what went wrong. Maybe the fact that Polydor was a foreign company and didn't understand the way Americans made or bought records had something to do with it.

Whatever the reasons, when my records didn't sell as well as they used to, Polydor crossed a line with me that I couldn't tolerate. It had been spelled out quite specifically in my contract that I would retain creative control of my records, but the Rifkins ignored that and, thinking they knew better than me, started to remix them. Why? In a sentence, even though they had, in effect, made me my own A and R man—the artist and repertoire executive who is really in charge of what finally gets put on a record—I got the creepy feeling that I was too Black for their mainstream tastes, which meant, I guess, I wasn't enough of a man for them to think I would know, or care, about what they were doing to my music. Or to me.

Almost from the get-go, they wanted to mix me down in every way—musically, rhythmically, commercially, *racially*. They really wanted more Elvis Presley and less James Brown. I had a song, "The Payback," that I wrote for the movie *Hell Up in Harlem*, but the label decided it wasn't "funky" enough. *What?* Not funky enough? I *invented* funky! I ought to at least have known what it sounded like! Against their wishes I released it the way I wanted to, and sure enough it went to number one on the R & B charts. So much for the geniuses at Polydor. However, even with that big hit, for the next two years there remained little support for me from my new label.

And there was something else that bothered me. I had strong suspicions, later proved, that all the money that was due to me was simply not coming my way. There were shenanigans going on that, I'm afraid, are common to the music industry. After all the years of being so careful, and learning the ins and outs of the business under the tutelage of Mr. Nathan, I was now on my own and becoming increasingly unhappy. There was no other way I could look at things except to know that I was in a bad situation.

The company wasn't smart enough to realize that if you have a happy artist, he or she will produce more hit records and therefore more money. If you rip him off, economically and in terms of his power and influence, you will kill his creative spark, and get less quality product; in the long run, you will lose.

Which is exactly what happened. I had no desire to make any more records for Polydor, other than the absolute minimum I had to deliver. They had forgotten one thing in all their sophisticated glory—I had already proved I could stop a riot, as when Dr. King was murdered. But I could also start one if I needed to.

As always seemed to happen, whenever I was too wrapped up in my business, real life would sneak up on me and land a rabbit punch to my heart. Just as I was getting ready to take on Polydor, I was blindsided by one of the worst personal tragedies one could have. What the label could never do—bring me to my knees—God did, by taking away the life of my son.

Teddy was my most talented offspring. He could sing and dance, and hold his own even against me. He even had his own group, Teddy Brown and the Torches, and whenever I saw them perform, I truly believed that I was watching my living legacy up there onstage. And then, in the space of a single phone call, he was gone.

I received the bad news on June 13, 1973. Teddy had been killed on the New York State Thruway about a hundred miles north of Albany. He wasn't even driving. Two other boys were with him, and apparently it was early in the morning and they might have been driving all night. The fellow behind the wheel fell asleep. The car went off the shoulder down an embankment, and all three of the passengers, including my Teddy, were killed instantly.

I was on my knees with grief. I cried, both for the crushing loss and because I had never had the chance to say good-bye to my little boy. Teddy was special, in the way that creative children are. He wasn't a particularly good student, and sometimes I think the system has no room for his kind of personality and talent. We had had some problems because he didn't want to stay in school. That tore me up inside. Here I was, the champion of Black youngsters, urging them to stay in school and get an education. I must have influenced thousands of boys and girls in my day, but tragically, I couldn't convince my own son to do the same. Perhaps because of my insistence, Teddy became rebellious, and for whatever reasons, I don't really know why, he began to act out his rebellion by passing bad checks. The police were starting to close in on him and I was eager to help him, but I couldn't, until it was too late.

All I can say is that Teddy came from a broken home, as I did, and for a lot of years I carried that guilt on my shoulders because I knew all too well what it meant to have a father who was never there, and I should have been able to handle the situation better. The difference between Teddy and me was that I had a special gift for music that got me through. Teddy had talent, too, but he didn't have enough time to see it blossom. In a way, his death seemed a kind of punishment for me that I could never be pardoned or paroled from, or a sin I could never properly atone for. His death became my ultimate life sentence.

Once again, there was nothing else I could do but go back to work.

The only problem was, work didn't necessarily want me back. There was a new sound in the air, and it was just about the opposite of everything I had come to stand for in music.

It was called disco.

TEN

PEOPLE'S TASTE IN POPULAR MUSIC HAD UNDERGONE a major shift in the seventies. No longer was it the politically charged force that it had once been in the sixties. Because disco was taking over, Polydor tried to get me to record something in that style with the hopes we might capture a share of the market. Although I wasn't particularly into the sound, the truth was that I had recorded every one of those rhythms and beats before in my own music, without the disco label attached because it hadn't as yet existed under that name.

To me, the music itself had not really changed all that much through the years. I had been performing what was arguably the first disco song, "Sex Machine," in one form or another in my shows since the early seventies (before releasing it as a single in 1975). Throughout the so-called Decade of Disco, and again today with all the dance music around in the clubs, "Sex Machine" is almost always a part of any hip DJ's playlist. Young people still love to dance to it, which I can understand. It's got all the ingredients of classic disco—rhythm, lyrics, bass.

There was, however, much more than just a musical change taking place in America. Politics had undergone a major shift as well, a change that affected everyone, from the protester on the street to topflight entertainers.

It was in the early seventies that I first met Marlon Brando, who I still consider one of the greatest cultural touchstones in America. He had been part of a growing community of White performers who stood solidly and proudly on the side of Black equality, not just in show business, but in every aspect of life in America. At one rally, I walked up to him and shook his hand and thanked him for all that he had done for this country. He was humble, as I knew he would be, and at that moment I felt that we were somehow partners in a small but powerful army of entertainers who used success for more than building up our bank accounts. He was as important an inspiration to me as any musician I'd ever heard. I'll never forget the moment when I told him that. He started crying right in front of me, out of sheer gratitude.

It was also about this time that I had the good fortune to meet Jerry Lewis, when he had a weekly show on network

TV. I remember he wanted me to do a skit and that worried me. I don't do that kind of thing—I'm strictly a singer and a dancer. I went to his office, knocked on the door, and heard him bark from the other side for me to come in. I did. First, I thanked him for having me on, and then I told him I wasn't comfortable with the skit he wanted me to do. "That's all right," he said, and put his arm around me. "I'll help you," he said. And he did. I appreciated that so much. I knew he did it because he wanted me to come off well on his show, and I did. It was his recognition of my fear that made it possible for him to reach out and guide me through what otherwise would have been an awkward and embarrassing experience for me. Mr. Lewis is one of the great fighters for the underdog.

And, of course, there is the great Kirk Douglas, who, like Mr. Brando, inspired me through his positive political activism. His strength and endurance reminded me once more of the major struggles still ahead in the war against racism in America, and that I had to reenlist as the one-man army called James Brown to fight in it. The only problem was, unlike the others, I was a badly wounded soldier and needed to fight this war on many fronts.

What I didn't realize was that another battle was raging, the one for my survival in a business that had all but changed before my very eyes. My dissatisfaction with my label, my inability to have a hit record, my not being able to receive airplay, my failure to book major venues—all of

it added up to a bottom line that carried with it a big minus sign. They say that when you're falling, you don't realize how far you've gone until you hit the ground. One day I
woke up, and I was covered in the rubble of my career.
And I could barely bring myself back up to a standing position. I decided to deconstruct everything about the
James Brown Revue, and put it back together again. The
way most people refurbish a home, I meant to rebuild my
career. And I was going to do it in the style of relevance.
The point was, an irrelevant James Brown could not carry
the weapons of cultural change on his shoulders. I had to
mean something as an entertainer in order to mean something to them as a cultural influence.

The first step was finding a way to reinvigorate my talent, something to hang my musical hat on, something even
more muscular and intense than what I already did. I
made my shows more elaborate to match the glitterball
times. I choreographed the passion of my soul so that it
took over the center-stage spotlight. Once I redecorated
my show, new music started pouring out of me. Suddenly,
I was writing new songs every minute, just for the *funk* of
it. Sometimes I could even create new music right onstage, during my show, after which I would have to run off,
round up some of the boys and drive directly to the nearest
studio to get it all down before I forgot any of the parts. I'd
play all the backgrounds for them so they could hear each
of the harmonies I was after separately, and I'd do the

same thing for the instruments. I was like a percolator boiling over with hot new ideas, wanting to express myself through this new idiom of my music.

Even so, there were some critics who thought that I had sold out, and that this wasn't the kind of music I was supposed to be making.

Supposed to be making?

Then how was it, I wondered, that my new records had brought me back to the top of the charts?

One thing I was aware of was how funk tended to draw more heavily from Black audiences than the mixed ones I was used to playing for, especially in the northern part of the country. That was fine with me. I rediscovered the joy of performing for largely Black audiences. I used to kid around a lot and tell my friends that I would rather play for Black people from the streets of the ghettos, or for prison audiences, than for those special invited foreign diplomats and high official elitists at the White House I always seemed to be called upon to entertain. That is not to say that I had anything against the country or its leaders, but that, to me, my own people were just as important, just as special, and just as worthy as anybody else in the country, including, if not more so than, presidents and senators. The circle of my journey back to myself was finished.

In 1972 I was offered a gig that was to change my life in the most unexpected way. I signed on to do the music for a film called *Black Caesar*, which was set in Harlem and had to do with the so-called Black Mafia. It was a kind of blaxpoitation film, as they called them at the time. During the recording of the soundtrack someone jokingly referred to me as the "Godfather of Soul." The name stuck, and that is the real and only reason why, no matter what anybody else claims to say or know, I am known to this day by that title.

During the making of the movie, I became even more politically engaged, and more visible in my activism. There was a national election coming up and I let it be known that I was leaning toward supporting Richard Nixon for re-election. I got a lot of pressure from his people to do so. I believe they felt my endorsement was as good a way as any to reach Black voters, which Mr. Nixon never had many of. It was around this time that Sammy Davis Jr. posed for that famous shot of him hugging the president. Not only did he get a lot of flack for it in the Black community, *but so did I!* A lot of people, both Black and White, tended to confuse the two of us, and thought it was *me* hugging the president.

I still believe supporting Nixon is one of the best things I have ever done, because it brought a Black presence into what had been an almost exclusively all-White administration, and did it in a positive and uplifting manner. Yet because of it, public resentment for me shot to an all-time high. Even my personal manager, Mr. Charles Bobbit, took me aside one day and very seriously asked if I had any idea what I was doing. I told him not to worry—it was the right move.

I remember a few years later when Mr. Jimmy Carter was running against Mr. Ronald Reagan, Mr. Bobbit asked me who I was voting for this time, and I told him, without skipping a beat, "President Nixon." He cracked up laughing. "You know you're still crazy!" he said.

"Wait until I run!" I told him.

In November 1972, Mr. Nixon remained in the White House, and to thank me for my support he invited the band and me to play at his inauguration. I surprised everyone, from Mr. Nixon to Mr. Bobbit, when I politely but firmly declined. People don't remember that. Six months later, in May of 1973, when I played the Apollo, for the first time ever in my life I was met with organized protests *from my fans*!

At every show Black people carried signs outside the venues calling me NIXON LOVER or JAMES BROWN NIXON CLOWN or GET THE CLOWN OUT OF TOWN. I was, to say the least, saddened by them. These were my people and I had tried to help them. I had, after all, captured the ear of a president who was not all that in touch and maybe not all that interested in the plight of ghetto Blacks in America. Everyone was not as well off as Sammy Davis Jr., or Sidney Poitier, or me. I thought I had created an opportunity to get our message heard in the White House, and on an intimate, one-to-one basis. Didn't that mean anything to my own people? I thought it had to.

Unfortunately, the opposite was true. Not only were Black people offended by my friendship with the president—so were White people. Because of their taking offense, few White radio stations would play my music and some Black stations wouldn't touch it either. As a result, I lost my only other direct connection to my people besides my live shows. It was a high price I paid for exercising the supposedly guaranteed freedoms I enjoyed as an American citizen, for having a mind and an opinion of my own, and not being afraid to express what was on it. I have always told audiences and interviewers alike, if you want to know who James Brown really is, just listen to his music. The problem now was gaining access to it. I began to feel that something must be very wrong with our notion of freedom of speech, if what we believe in can't be heard.

Don't you agree?

The fallout from my association with the president continued to do damage to me, both personally and professionally. It has since been proved that J. Edgar Hoover, with who knows whose permission, had a mandate to prevent the rise in America of a new Black leader. All of us who were Black and in the public eye were put under intense surveillance, harassed by the IRS, and subjected to all forms of underhanded activities to discredit us in an effort to take away our hard-earned money, and therefore our potential political power. No matter what it took.

Sure enough, I suddenly had new troubles with the IRS. Out of nowhere—or at least it seemed that way to me—they claimed I owed four million dollars in back taxes, which was crazy. There's no other word for it (except maybe prejudicial, vindictive, politically motivated, etc.). In America, everybody has the right to have a message to bring to the table. The only problem is, certain people don't get the chance to come to that table! So what happens? They congregate among themselves, angry and driven, and sometimes bad things happen. They usually know what they're talking about, the proof and the strength of their message being in direct conflict with the efforts to suppress it by those who don't want anyone to hear it.

Let me tell you a story about the IRS and me. I had made a fortune from song royalties, I think, and had put a million dollars or so in the bank. I was having a great night's sleep for the first time in a long time when, early the next morning, Mr. Bobbit called me on the phone. He was frantic. "The IRS has taken all of your money!" he said.

I looked at the phone, then put it back to my ear. "Is that what you woke me up for? Call me when something important happens!" And with that, I went back to sleep for a good, long, peaceful rest despite all the difficulties the IRS caused me. I was never going to let them win. Money would never rule me or bring me to my knees, or stop me from thinking, eating, breathing, writing—or *dreaming*.

The next thing I knew, the IRS and the FCC had taken away the rest of my few remaining radio stations in order to satisfy that tax lien. In doing so, they also happened to silence one of the strongest and most vital voices that spoke directly to America's Black community.

Then they took away the other, smaller plane I had bought, and that meant taking away part of my livelihood. I was at a level of show business success where a private plane was no longer a luxury, but a necessity. It gave me three extra days out of the week to be able to travel to new cities to do shows, and it also increased my downtime, which is necessary to keep a show at the level of energy I did. Most often it is commercial flying that defeats most performers. After a while they just can't take the energy-draining hassle and the expense of public traveling anymore. Taking my plane away was like taking my microphone away; I simply couldn't do my job without either.

It didn't stop there. After the IRS took away my bank account, they appropriated my last house, the one on the White side of Augusta.

Meanwhile, the very same issues that had broken up my first marriage were now threatening my second. I was away so much of the time, a situation now made worse by my losing my plane, that Deedee was, by necessity, increasingly home alone, having to take care of our home and the kids without me. She knew me well enough to know that long absences meant that I would revert to the realities of life on the road. Even though I was a married man, I still had a single man's urges. To try to reassure her that my heart was in the right place, next to hers, I decided to install a "hotline" telephone for her so that she could get ahold of me whenever she wanted to, and so we could talk to each other whenever either of us needed to. But it wasn't enough to overcome her resentment over my being away all that time. While I thought I was doing the right thing, she felt the phone was my way of trying to control her. As time wore on, Deedee began to see that for her our marriage as one very well-appointed gilded cage. In truth, I was not happy living two half-lives: a husband and a father who was never there, and a performer who felt he had to be. My unhappiness spread like a cancer through the foundation of our marriage. There's no getting around the fact that when two people are not physically together, they begin to lead individual lives.

Inevitably, this led to a final breakup. It felt to me like I had once more gone to Hell and back. It was difficult, but I got through it, even if it did leave me even more gun-shy than ever in the area of marriage. There has since been a lot of talk about the breakup, both publicly and privately, but the heart of the matter was that Deedee couldn't take the reality of the show business life. Some things aren't meant to last forever. I understand and accept that and I think she did, too.

Alone once more, I turned all my energies and concentration back onto saving my career. I worked my rear end off, mostly performing in clubs and small arenas, but it seemed that no matter how much I made, it was not enough. Thankfully, I was never into owning a lot of extraneous, ego-boosting "things." All I needed was a pair of good shoes, some healthful food, a nice car, a plane to get me to the next show, and the kind of clothes that made me look my best onstage. But there are always taxes to pay, equipment to replace, ex-wives and children to support, and lawsuits. Countless lawsuits, nearly all of them "nuisance" type. All celebrities get hit with them, but they still have to be defended and that costs a great deal of money.

The price of innocence remains high in America. Believe me, I know what I'm talking about. For someone in my position, with my earning potential and my notoriety, it is possible to go from poor to rich and still feel that you've done something worthwhile. It's much more difficult to return to being rich once you've lost everything and have become poor, because when you're in the public eye there's nowhere to hide your pride on the way down.

And on top of everything else, there was what I call the

"woman" situation, which became relevant for me once again after my divorce. If you're a Black man and you're seen in public with a White woman in the South, it's going to cost you. Not just in the expected ways, but in *every* way. I could be driving along the boulevard and a police officer would haul me over to check my license without ever giving me a reason why. If I happened to be with a Black woman, and my license was good, they always let me go, still without an explanation. But if I was with a White woman, they always found a reason to run me in, and ring the municipal cash register. In those days it cost me an awful lot to keep my freedom if I had the audacity to socialize with a White woman in the South. And let me tell you, no matter what you might think, it's the same way to this day, brother, to this very day. They will always find a way to get to me when they don't like something I've done, justice and James Brown be damned.

ELEVEN

ELVIS PRESLEY DIED IN AUGUST 1977, AND THAT HIT me hard. Even as I was trying to regain my footing in the mainstream, the loss of which had drained me of most of my possessions, my second marriage, all of my money, but never my desire to entertain, here was poor Elvis, found dead on his toilet seat, unable to find any kind of peace within himself. I always identified with Elvis, and personally liked him very much. We had both come out of the poor South, and each, in our own way, had at various times in our careers been kept apart from the people and things we loved most: our music and the connection to our audiences.

The month before Elvis died, I played the Apollo. Even though I was supposed to be "washed-up" in the business, thanks to disco, and all my so-called "legal" issues, which I considered nothing more than the usual government harassment, I sold the house out for the entire run. For a while it seemed as if the good old days had returned. That is, until the final Sunday night performance when I received a backstage visit from a federal marshal who had a bench warrant for my arrest on contempt of court charges, stemming from myriad civil lawsuits, and in particular, this one having to do with some unresolved financial matters pertaining to one of my old radio stations. I was taken directly from the Apollo to a Baltimore jail.

During that incarceration, I thought about chucking the whole entertainment gig for the first time in my life. It wasn't as if I had never been in jail before. Ever since I was a boy, the only drapes I recognized were the steel ones that hung in front of my windows. Only a few months earlier, I had performed at a concert in Knoxville, Tennessee, the heart of the Old South, and after the show a gang of police was waiting for all of us in the alley behind the theater.

For no reason that any of us could imagine other than sheer redneck hatred, they started beating on the boys. I had a licensed .38 that I carried for protection in my pocket, but God must have been protecting me that night because none of those police ever hit me. Had they, even once, I would have taken out my pistol and surely been shot dead on the spot.

I was arrested and thrown into a jail cell, and all the while the .38 was sitting in my pocket. Southern justice was such that they hadn't bothered to search me, let alone charge me for anything. Instead they just threw me and the others into a tank. The eventual and trumped-up charge was "inciting a riot." That's what made the papers, and that's what people thought happened: James Brown was out of control again!

Fortunately for me, I was able to get out of that situation, and when I did, I vowed to never again find myself at the mercy of those who held the big lock and key. And yet, here I was, once again sitting alone and cold in a padlocked prison cell. No single arrest had ever broken my spirit—now, however, the collective experience of having my freedom taken away yet again was almost more than I could bear. I started wondering if I had finally lost it, if they had finally won. Maybe they were never going to allow me to be "James Brown" again.

Fortunately, although I didn't have a lot of money at the time, I had a wealth of connections in the bank of my social and cultural experiences. I had made great, loyal friends in the civil rights movement, and now, when I needed something in return, one of them stepped up to help me. He was the great civil attorney William Kunstler, and he was a man whose commitment to justice for *all* was more than a mere slogan. He put his jurisprudence where his mouth was, and the only fee he was interested in when it came to the underdog was the satisfaction of proving that the system could work for everyone.

He took on my case, got me out of jail, and managed to quickly work out a reasonable settlement with the government over that lingering problem, and made it possible for me to return to work. What particularly struck me was that here was a White man who could have made all the money in the world as a lawyer, but instead, he chose to defend people like me—Black, disenfranchised, and in need of what he had. In a way, I felt that we had each given the other something through our lifework—I had enriched his world through my music, and he had returned value to mine with his legal skills. That was America at its best to me.

Still, I had to eat a lot of humble pie. And the truth of the matter was that I was now free in every sense of the word. I had nothing. I had to start over from the beginning. For the next couple of years I played small rock clubs I never would have considered even ten years earlier, tiny holes in the wall that could barely hold a hundred people. After my experience at the Copa, I told myself I would never compromise myself again. Now, though, I didn't think I had the right—or the means—to turn this kind of work down. So every night I gave it everything I had, even if the stages were sometimes not much larger than the trays that the waitresses carried as they served. I brought as many musicians as I could squeeze into those venues, and they had to literally rub shoulders to play their instruments.

And yet it was those very clubs that held the key to my

eventual comeback. During one of my many swings
through New York City, I played the Lone Star in Green-
wich Village (an ironic name for a club featuring James
Brown, I thought at the time). During that gig, two up-
and-coming comics came down, caught the show, and afterward offered me yet one more shot at salvation—both
personal and professional. Their names were John Belushi
and Dan Ackroyd. They were hot because of the success
of their new TV show, *Saturday Night Live*. They wanted
to make a movie based on the Blues Brothers, one of their
most popular skits, and they wanted me to play a part in it.

The role they had in mind was that of a gospel preacher.
I shot my scene in a re-created church on a back lot at
Universal Studios in Los Angeles. The movie, directed by
John Landis, proved to be a huge hit, and was the single
most important factor in returning me to the spotlight.
The success of the film gave me the popularity and the le-
gitimacy to return to the big venues, the arena circuit, and
to emerge from the media-imposed cloak of invisibility
and appear again on network television.

The film opened and proved to be such a bit hit that
network doors finally parted for me again and I received an
invitation to appear on *Saturday Night Live*. After that
came the *Tomorrow* show with Tom Snyder, the *Mike
Douglas Show*, and a host of others. As *The Blues Brothers*
began to play internationally, I was invited to each of the
countries it opened in, beginning with Germany and Italy,

and eventually I managed to tour all over the world. By 1982, midway through the first term of President Ronald Reagan, I was finally back on top! The circle of my journey had taken yet another revolution.

In February of that year, I appeared on *Solid Gold*, an important nationally syndicated rock-and-roll show, one of the few that had managed to stay on the air in the form of television/radio. A host, or DJ, would introduce an act, the performers would come out and play a song, and then the DJ would return to introduce the next act. These were the last days before the arrival of MTV, and rock-and-roll shows were quickly fading. But *Solid Gold* held on and was able to make a difference, and I was happy to be asked to appear on the show.

Another reconnection I was able to make that for me was equally important was with my love life. During my appearance on *Solid Gold*, I met a beautiful woman by the name of Adrianne, who happened to be working on the set that day. We met, our eyes locked, our souls touched. By the end of the taping, without having to say or do anything, we both knew that we were in love. I've always believed that the heart is powered by God's lightning. It only takes an instant for the bolt to hit you. The feelings that remain can last a lifetime.

Unfortunately, also on the set that day was her ex-husband, who had come to get some paperwork settled between them. Someone warned me to stay away from Adrianne because her ex was the jealous type, and there might be a little trouble if I pursued her. Now trouble was always the last thing I wanted, but Adrianne had become the first. As it happened, I was scheduled to have dinner that night with the Reverend Al Sharpton and his wife. I asked one of my backup singers to quietly ask Adrianne if she would like to join us. She came back smiling and told me that Adrianne had said yes.

And so it was that we began a very special courtship. Adrianne was not like a lot of the other women I had known. She had dated only one other man besides the one she married, and that other man happened to be Elvis Presley. She was special. She had a very calm and gentle demeanor. As we started to date, whenever I'd get angry at someone, or feel the weight of race coming down on my shoulders, she'd say, softly, "James, don't say that . . . don't hate anybody . . . don't feel that way about anybody. If you can't say anything good, better not to say anything at all. . . ." And it always worked. I'd feel the tension dissipate from my body and my mind. I believed I had finally found a woman who understood the power of true love.

Adrianne was from the West Coast, so I made it my business to come calling for her there. I'd pick her up and take her all over California to see the places I most enjoyed, like Sausalito and San Diego. It was going to be difficult, but I was determined not to let the great distance between our two homes interfere with our love.

As it turned out, I didn't have to. Shortly after we began

dating, she took a job in New York City doing makeup on a soap opera, which necessitated her to commute from coast to coast. Soon enough, she began to complain of all the travel time. That's when I offered what I thought was a pretty good alternative. "Give up your house and your job and come live with me," I told her. A week later she was unpacking her bags at my home.

We had a lot of wonderful things in common. She was multicultural, so was I. She was part Italian, African, Jewish, and Hispanic, which seemed to perfectly complement my Indian, African, and a touch of so many other genes. In other words, she was a rainbow and so was I, something I really liked about us. We could feel at home together in both the White and the Black world (and sometimes in neither). She also came from a broken home, so we both knew how to respect the emotional remnants of the shattered childhoods each of us had had. And of course it didn't hurt any that her tastes were absolutely contemporary, allowing her to work on things like my hair, my wardrobe, my lifestyle, and just about everything else about me that needed it.

However, no sooner did she move into my home than problems began. A *lot* of problems. I was living now in a small green house I had found in nearby South Carolina, just across the Savannah River from Augusta; the house was built on and surrounded by an ancient Indian burial ground. One of the reasons I loved the place so much was because I could feel the presence of, and was able to honor, the souls of my ancient dear departed every day.

My relationship with my ancestors was beautiful—my relationship with Adrianne would unfortunately be less so. The first thing that went wrong was when Adrianne told everyone her name was Rodriguez, so she wouldn't have a hard time dealing with being part Italian or part Jewish in the deep South. It wasn't until much later on that she was able to even hint that she was something other than Black.

Racism cuts wide and it cuts deep. To me, it was like all the other problems people have in this country when they're a little different. The clash of color, the clash of religion, the clash of political affiliation, the clash of those who have money against those who don't. This economic and social form of multiculturalism is both dangerous and primitive, and does nothing to promote a harmonious country made up of citizens from all the others. From the start, I kept telling Adrianne that we had to settle into this neighborhood on *the good foot*! But it would prove easier said than done.

I didn't realize how difficult it was going to be for someone who had grown up on the enlightened West Coast, surrounded by sophisticated show business people, where race was never really an issue. Suddenly, here she was in the middle of America's past, under the microscope of a society where anything that was the least bit different from what they knew, wanted, or expected caused problems for everybody.

Adrianne didn't look like anyone else in South Carolina, she didn't talk like anyone else, she didn't dress like Southern ladies were "supposed" to, and she was living with me, South Carolina's most celebrated rock-and-roll jailbird. The cards were stacked against us from the moment of the first deal.

TWELVE

ONE SUCCESS WILL GO A LONG WAY TO ELIMINATE A lot of failures. After my appearance in *The Blues Brothers*, the rest of my career seemed to fall back into place. In 1985, after completing all of my obligations to Polydor, I signed on with the Scotti brothers, Johnnie and Vin, and their label, which was a subsidiary of CBS, for recording management duties. My feeling was that the Scotti brothers saw me the way I saw myself: on the other side of disco, still being a contemporary R & B act capable of making the charts. Polydor, on the other hand, had invested everything they had in disco.

And so I signed with the Scotti brothers from a position of power, after my comeback. I had first met them while making the movie *The Blues Brothers*, and it was because of the success I enjoyed making it that we all decided to continue to work together and formalize our relationship. Thanks to Mr. Belushi and Mr. Ackroyd, I had a small part in the movie.

I soon began to appear in a number of movies, including *Doctor Detroit*, where I sang "Get Up offa That Thing," and then *Rocky IV*, where I had the opportunity to introduce a brand-new song—"Living In America." That became my first really big hit in years, and something of an anthem for the eighties.

I have to give the Scotti brothers some credit for the success of that song. They certainly had the right idea about the direction my career needed to go in. They respected me and what I could do, and after "Living in America," I had a string of hit tunes that included "Unreal" and "Static," both of which landed on the charts at the same time. I also cut a couple of sides with Aretha Franklin.

I was also getting regular bookings in the main rooms of Las Vegas, a far cry from the Lone Star. I was happy about that, but despite my live appearances, my movies, and my hit singles, I still wasn't feeling the old heat from within the industry. It's possible the Scotti brothers just didn't have enough juice at the time, but I didn't think that was the problem. I believed then (and do now) that there were simply too many organized forces at work within the government who had decided I was still too dangerous to be allowed back into the mainstream. I felt I was being punished—some might call it blacklisted—and what was even worse, I had no idea who was actually behind it all.

As a result—and whether or not it was true or I was being paranoid, and looking for excuses as to why I wasn't doing even better—I became angrier and angrier and more difficult to be around.

Predictably, things got worse in my marriage, as my frustrations grew. Adrianne had always had had a calming effect; she had the magic touch, and could defuse me at will. Now I was the one who was starting to agitate her. That was not a good thing. On top of that, money was still a problem. And unable to face the frustrating realities of my life, I began to drink more heavily than I ever had before, and for the first time in my life regularly used hard drugs.

As I've said, I was no angel. When you're in the music business, certain things are always available: women, booze, and drugs the foremost of them. I may have had a taste of each now and again, but I was always afraid that if I crossed a certain line, I'd wind up like Elvis or poor John Belushi, or Little Willie, or any number of great talents who were brought down by their own self-destructive behavior. Until that time, I had always been able to keep that demon at bay. However, the struggle against temptation is one that never ends. All it takes is the dropping of your guard one time. I let that happen, and while I was in a stupor, the Devil came and tried to take my entire world away. Here's how.

In December 1988, I was driving my pickup truck when

suddenly I found myself being pursued by officers investigating a charge brought by Adrianne that I had shot up her car with a gun and gone after her with a tire iron. After the fight with my wife, blind with fury and high as a kite, I took my shotgun with me into a meeting I had called in my office complex just over the state line in Augusta, Georgia, and, I guess, scared the daylights out of everybody.

What can I say? The whole thing was an absolute out-of-focus nightmare. After the meeting, I was driving home, when suddenly I saw a police roadblock up ahead of me. I simply went around it, not thinking for a second they could possibly be after me. I thought somebody must have robbed ten banks the way they were set up with their lights flashing and their weapons drawn. All I was doing was getting out of the way so that the police could do their job, never dreaming their job was to catch me.

It wasn't until one of their cars, an unmarked one at that, came up alongside and asked me to pull over that I understood who the police were after. So I pulled over. All they had to do was ask! An officer then got out of his vehicle and came over to mine. We talked for a little while, nothing unusual, until he suddenly asked me to get out. I said, "Should I get out on the driver's side?" and he said, "No, slide over and use the passenger door."

As I began to do so, another officer came up and smashed in the right front window with his nightstick and foot, as if he were trying to get into a burning building to save someone from a fire. I couldn't believe what was happening. There was shattered glass everywhere, sirens going off, and what appeared to me to be a sudden and full-scale attack, all coming after I had voluntarily pulled over and had been calmly talking with the first officer.

Then, I guess to make sure that I couldn't get away, one of the officers fired eight bullets into the front two wheels of my truck, and another fifteen rounds into the chassis. Bullets were flying everywhere and I thought for sure I was going to die in the cross fire. I held my breath waiting for one of the bullets to hit me. When it was over, or so I thought, I thanked God I was still alive, until I saw the officer who had fired start to reload.

Now, look, if a man, any man, empties a gun into my car and then reloads, I don't have to be a rocket scientist to figure out why. I'm out of there. I don't care *who* it is. As far as I was concerned, he wasn't putting those bullets into his gun's chamber for the rest of the tires, but for my heart. I jumped back in the car and gunned her for all she was worth, driving on the rims, desperate to save my life.

And that, my friends, is what the police later described as resisting arrest.

Yeah, it was resisting arrest all right, by a Black man in the South with White officers shooting up his car and reloading their weapons, and no witnesses anywhere. Resisting arrest from some armed men about to make my head match the tires they had just shot full of holes.

I didn't get very far before I lost control of the truck and ran off the road. Ironically, I landed in a ditch about a mile from where I had first been arrested as a boy.

The police pulled me out, sent for an ambulance, and when it was determined that I had not been seriously hurt, they took me into custody. When I was brought before the judge, I refused to plead guilty to anything, and because of my defiance, correct or otherwise, I was convicted of aggravated assault and failure to stop for a blue light, meaning a police car. The simple truth is, I had run for my life, and for that, and nothing else, at the age of fifty-five, I was handed a six-year sentence in the Georgia State Penitentiary.

To be sure, some of the things that I did that day were not very nice, but I never did anything the police said I did. It was simply a vengeance sentence, made worse by my celebrity. Because I was a famous Black performer, busted roadside in the South, I had to pay the price. They wanted the whole world to see how "right" they were whenever they said how lawless, violent, and dangerous Southern Blacks were.

Or maybe it was just my music that scared them to death!

I still have that truck behind my house, all shot up, sitting right next to all my other vehicles. It serves as a reminder, and a warning to me, of how many different types of slave shackles there really are in this man's world. The one thing it doesn't do is remind me of my "lapsed morality," or keep me on any guilt trip, because I can't feel bad about something I didn't do.

I don't accept the version that the police issued as the truth of what happened that day. I don't regard the police as the Highest Authority. I answer for my actions to the Holy Spirit, and whatever He judges, *that's* what I believe.

And as for my reputation, that's a really funny one, because at the time *I didn't have a reputation!* Not down south, or at least not one that was any good, anyway. I never have. Regardless of how many people I've helped during the years, who I've put into business or sent to school, no matter how much money I've brought into Augusta by my presence there, the numerous jobs I've created—all of it—I'm still considered something of an embarrassment to my hometown because of incidents such as these.

I want everyone, White and Black (and all the colors in between), from everwhere to know this about me: I have never and will never go against the system. Our country is the best. No one has ever been able to successfully challenge our society or bring down our system of law and order. And in that system, I feel that I have always been a productive citizen, looking to make people feel better via my music, and hoping to somehow influence the bad ones and make them feel better about the world they live in and themselves.

That's why, for me, being put in jail for 2.5 years before I was paroled was not a punishment in the traditional sense. I wasn't arrested—I was *rescued*. I wasn't doing anything good out there, for myself or for my wife at the time. I was into some bad things and in need of help. I call my time in prison the poor man's Medicare!

All the time I was on the inside, I tried to keep a positive frame of mind, and was determined to improve myself so that when I got out, I could reenter the system with even more self-assurance and self-pride. It was, in many ways, a much-needed break that rescued me from the crazy merry-go-round of booze and drugs that I was a passenger on. I was tired, my resistance was low, and I needed a place to get myself together. Prison gave me that. Only there was I was finally able to get off the substances I knew I shouldn't have been using, eat the right foods three times a day, get regular exercise, go to bed early and wake up early, and most of all, get back into the head of the real James Brown, who I had been away from for too long.

I knew that I was no Little Willie John, that I hadn't done the things he had, and I wasn't going to die on the inside. In fact, every day I was there I got stronger, and I vowed that when I got out, I'd work harder than I ever had, and be bigger than at any previous time in my career. It was that vow, that commitment to myself that kept me going, day after day, until the time came when the Man opened those big iron gates and I was able to walk back into the heavenly sunshine of my life.

On the other hand, those 2.5 years were nothing but Hell for those who locked me up. First of all, they knew that I was not guilty of anything but my own weaknesses, and my "crimes" had nothing to do with the law. By incarcerating me, the authorities only proved how wrong they were, and how right I was. They became the snakes outside the door. I believe that in the eyes of the rest of the world, it made them look very bad to lock up someone like me, at my age, with my stature, a famous Black man, in my own hometown. I remember when I was being taken away, some reporter asked me how I felt, if I thought there was any racial motivation to what was going down. I held up my shackled wrists, smiled, and said, "Do you see these handcuffs? They're called America." I think that summed it up pretty well.

Almost from the day I was incarcerated, a Free James Brown movement began, and I have to say it felt totally gratifying that there were so many people in this country, Black *and* White, who were outraged by what was being done to me. Locking me up for something no White man would have gone to prison for did nothing so much as turn me into the newest martyr for civil rights. Everyone on the inside instantly became my friend, and took very good care of me. All of us were bound together and focused on a single shared goal.

Freedom.

The day of my release, I hit the street running, aching to get back to work. Even before I got out, Mr. Bobbit had seen to it that my calendar was loaded with dates, and for the next two years I worked diligently to restore my reputation (and my wallet). People came out to see me and the word quickly spread that the Godfather of Soul was alive and kicking. And kicking I was! I gave what I think were the best shows of my life those two years, because I was happy, I was in great shape, I was free, and I was back onstage, where I belonged. Nothing, I thought to myself, could stop me now.

Until something did.

My wife, Adrianne, had wanted to get some minor cosmetic surgery. She had had cosmetic surgery before, and it had always gone off without a hitch. She checked in to a hospital, and during the procedure something went terribly wrong. She never awakened from the anesthetic, and died on the operating table. This completely shattered me and I felt a profound loss as deeply affecting as when my son was killed.

I'm not going to pretend that my marriage to Adrianne was perfect, or smooth, or idyllic, or any of that. In truth, like my two previous attempts at matrimony, it was rough, turbulent, and at times it could get maddening. But I loved her and she loved me. Adrianne was a good woman and did not deserve to die that way. Nobody does. I was sick over it, and if I hadn't been as strong as I was, I'm certain I would have gone down for the count.

The only thing I knew how to do that could get me out of the despair was the thing I always did in tragic times such as these: I plunged myself back into work.

And that is exactly what I did. With a vengeance.

Fortunately for me, all during the time I had been incarcerated and for the following two years, an up-and-coming generation of rappers and hip-hoppers had suddenly discovered their musical roots, meaning the music of James Brown. God must have surely been looking out for me, especially in this, my time of sorrow, because by virtue of this new generation of Black performers and their search for something a little deeper, a little gutsier, a little more forceful and joyful than the disco and pop they had turned away from, they found something in my music they could identify with. It filled the bill for them perfectly and inspired everything from their melodies to their looks, moves, and onstage attitudes and for that of course I am both proud and grateful.

They took the fierce, positive pride that is the heart and soul of my music, and blended it with the anger they felt at injustice as well as the respect we all share as Black brothers and sisters, brewed it up into an attitude they called "nineties," and laid it over a funky beat infused with a new energy. They danced like I danced, only with a chorus of boys and girls behind them, and opened up the stage to a completely new kind of show spectacle.

But they knew and I knew that underneath it all was James Brown, who had taken them as babies from gospel to soul, from soul to funk, and now from funk to hip-hop. I became the most sampled artist of all time, the most inspirational Black performer in the business, the toughest kid to knock down. Again I have no one to thank for that but God.

THIRTEEN

IN 1990, I WAS ALL SET TO RESUME MY RECORDING AND touring career, and to get together again with Aretha Franklin to pick up where we had both left off, but I hadn't counted on one thing. Rap had not only entered the mainstream, but buried everything else in its wake.

I was not happy about this, and not just because of what it did to my own career. It troubled me how America saw rap as a clear reflection of its Black population. Not because of the rap itself, or the boys and girls making it—that was fine—but in the way the country was so eager to accept Blacks as "gangstas," without hearing any of the true social content of what the kids were singing about. There was a strong message to be taken, and it wasn't registering. Instead, people got distracted by the clothes, the girls, the cursing, and the playacting. It was too bad, because to Black kids, who, as always, had to look into the street to find out what was really happening, there was a clear message coming through and it wasn't pretty. What they were hearing in the official press, and on TV, made no sense to them. They didn't know what anybody was talking about.

That is not to say that I'm not down with everything that's going on in the business today. I like a lot of rap and hip-hop, but I find that the music industry is far more bizarre than the music itself right now, so unfair and so filled with people who don't know what they're doing that I wonder if anybody is really getting any kind of the fair shake they deserve. I know, when I was young and starting out, Mr. Nathan said the same thing about me—"He doesn't know what he's doing"—and let me record what I wanted to. If he hadn't, there would never have been a single of "Please Please Please" and most likely no "James Brown."

I want to be clear—I'm not saying young people today, the rappers, are victims, or that they don't know any better. They're running the show now, and we'll have to see what comes out of that, and if any of them can go the distance. If they do, then they were right on. But the truth remains that it is so difficult for them to be able to see day-to-day reality. The artist gets his music out of the air, out of the atmosphere—you can't see the inspiration, you can't touch it, it comes to you in your sleep, it comes when someone of authority in the community says the words "can't" or "don't" directed our way. It's everywhere and it's invisible, and that is what makes it all at once so accessible and so elusive.

I think I can take a little credit for influencing the beat of rap, based as it is on the old drums of passion, my personal combination of the drums of Africa and the drums of the American Indian, both of whom I claim a heritage from. I gave Black music a different sound, the one/three that much of rap is based on. I didn't have as much influence on the lyrics because I've always been against using bad words and antifemale images in music. The thing about rap that is so powerful is that it doesn't try to change people. It only gets them to listen, to consider, and to understand the world around them. It's more of a wake-up call for what people already know than a program of propaganda.

Although my music sounds nothing like today's rap and hip-hop, in many ways, it's exactly the same when it comes to the struggle that they represent. The style may be different; the message is the same. It becomes a different and more difficult struggle to be heard and accepted when you don't tone anything down. It becomes a danger. It awakens the sleeping giant, especially for a race that has been kept down by the majority of the populace and the government that runs it.

It is ironic to me that performers like Stevie Wonder and the late Ray Charles couldn't see what was all around them, but knew how it *felt* to be Black in America. Everyone could see them, but because they were blind, they saw in another way, without color, so to speak, and I think it made their creative journeys easier. The prejudice and hard times were out there; they just didn't have to confront them with their eyes open. Because they somehow escaped the in-your-face hatred, they were able to concentrate on the basics of their music, and it's these basics that the Black man has given the White man when it comes to musical entertainment. There's just no way around that. Unfortunately for some, the style that is in vogue today makes it all the more difficult for other, less forceful voices to have their impact.

Rap and hip-hop, as much as funk and soul, are all ultimately reflective musical forms. They hold a mirror up to the times, and if that reflection is distorted, it's not the glass that's the problem—it's the perception of the person looking.

As for me, I've always been a stylistic preacher, someone who wants to extend a hand to all races, all colors, both in America and around the world. I'm always ready to lend a hand, give advice, and offer encouragement. After all, I am the Godfather of Soul!

As long as rap is so pervasive right now, maybe it's worth another look. I'll let you in on a little secret. I believe—and a lot of people in the industry will know what I'm talking about—that a lot of the more tasteless aspects of rap is really part of a government conspiracy to destroy the integrity of Black music in America. Let me explain what I mean.

I firmly believe that Black music should never be "dirty." And if you think about it, how could it be, unless someone higher up was allowing it? The FCC controls the licensing of everything connected to broadcasting. If they don't want something on the air, it doesn't get on. Conversely, whatever material does make it on the airwaves is the material that they have deemed "appropriate." I believe a lot of the most anarchic, "dirty" songs that have made rap something it wasn't intended to be by Blacks were either something they were pressured by labels into recording, or actually products originated by some faction of the FCC to discredit all the artists who rap, and the audiences who buy it. Who else do you think has sanctioned all the playing of the worst of it on the air, constantly, so that White people could shake their heads and say, "See? *That's* what Black people are really all about. That's how they talk about their girlfriends and worse, their mamas. Instead of building their women up, they portray them as whores and sluts! And *that's* what they allow their children to listen to."

Where is all this going to lead? Rappers out there, I'm especially talking to you! *Listen to your Godfather!* I know some of you will think I'm crazy for even suggesting it, but please, maybe we shouldn't all be so quick to dismiss the words of a man who speaks from firsthand knowledge of the music business as well as firsthand experience dealing with the government. Somebody's lying to you somewhere, and that someone isn't me. Unfortunately, it appears to be the way things have come down, and why we need to get back to the roots of our music, our industry, and our souls. And the only way to do that is to return to the purity of our love for our music, and all the positive things that it represents for us.

Could I be the one to do it? Have I done it before? The answer to both questions is yes, at least it is today, but back in 1990 I had the creepy feeling that it was me, and not the industry, who had fallen out of the mainstream, and that was a sure sign that I was in trouble, that I had somehow lost my own sense of creativity. When in fact, the opposite was true—the mainstream had fallen out of me.

By then, I thought I had learned everything there was to know about the music industry, all the rules of the system. And then, without warning, everything changed again. It was like growing up being Fred Astaire and suddenly being told you had to go to dancing school to learn some new steps.

A lot of the early pioneers of rock, soul, and funk stood for different things. Some stood for sex, some for love, some for religion. I aligned myself early on with freedom. I was, in many ways, the Jackie Robinson of pop music, because of the incredible crossover I made without compromising my presentation. No one ever was able to get me to water down what I did, to make it more "palatable" to the mainstream.

Joe Louis was another figure who was all about freedom, especially when he won the championship. "Sugar" Ray Robinson was a ghetto hero who represented a way out to a lot of kids who looked up to him and saw the ability of a man of color to stand as tall, if not taller, than the White man. Harry Belafonte fought for his right to remain true to his heritage while becoming a mainstream star. With his open shirt, short hair, and starkly romantic image, he was quite startling when he first came along. A lot of people might not remember that back in the sixties when he had a TV special on one of the networks, he kissed Petula Clark, quite innocently, on the cheek, I believe, or maybe even just touched her hand, and it caused a major scandal along with a lot of outrage, particularly down south. Belafonte stood tall in the face of angry letters, death threats, and more. Like all the others, he was a hero to me, a Black man to be admired, one of many who helped change the culture of America and allowed a James Brown to take it to another level, paving the way for today's rappers to go even further down the line of acceptability.

Not that it was easy. The crossover didn't come overnight, although a lot of people forget the early years and think that I exploded onto the scene instantaneously. The long years of playing small clubs were difficult, especially for a young, uneducated Southern Black boy. I had to hone my craft while making sure that I didn't break any of the White man's rules and get my throat slit ear to ear, or get into trouble with any White women and be hanged for it by their boyfriends or uncles or fathers. It wasn't easy because, and I'm being completely honest with you, those paleface women were always in heat when they saw my show and were forever chasing me around every chance they got. Finding my voice, writing my songs, putting the right combination of players together, connecting with Mr. Nathan—all of that took time.

But I always had one goal in my sights, and that was freedom—my freedom, meant to represent and reflect all Black people's freedom. Even when I was nothing more than a musical Black moth, I knew one day that if I could hang in there, I'd emerge as a beautiful rainbow butterfly. That one day took years to get to. The intervening time was my form of education, my way of "earning" my experiences so that when I sat down to write my songs, I knew where I had come from and what I was talking about, and that it was real.

One of the problems I find with a lot of today's rap and R & B performers is that they haven't "lived" their lyrics. And because they haven't, they can't sing it like they lived it. They have no idea where their own styles or the roots of their music come from. That is crucial to why my music still works and lasts, while a lot of today's probably won't. I lived mine, and when I wrote it, I relived every emotional moment, high and low, and performed every night onstage as if it were happening all over again for the first time.

With too many of these new-style performers, they do the best they can, and are often quite entertaining, but they really don't have a clear model in their heads for their music. They're kind of feeling their way, and as a result their shows look too much like they've been handed to them by an expert; they're overchoreographed, and there's nothing behind the moves.

When I broke in, my dancing and movement onstage was as strong a social statement as it was a show business one. I was fighting racism, poverty, and all the issues that were the foundation for my music, along with love and good times. When I was coming up, certain songs turned my head completely around. I loved Anthony Newley's "What Kind of Fool Am I?", which Sammy Davis later on had such a big hit with. What a moment of self-examination and realization! *That's* a song. *"What kind of fool am I, who never fell in love..."* My problem, of course, was that I fell in love too many times, which was what made the song resonate so deeply in my soul. We're all fools for love in our own way, aren't we? We don't immediately know everything. We have to keep trying; otherwise we might as well not get out of bed in the morning, and if that's the case we'll be alone in it when we wake up.

Today, young performers tend to go directly for the center spotlight, often on the manufacturing and promotional skills of some label genius rather than on their own innate abilities, and the next thing they know, they're "stars." As a result, a lot of their music operates from the outside in, instead of the other way around. When I performed what I consider to be one of the forerunners to modern rap, it had a certain catch to it. *Take a Look at Those Cakes* was all about women, and clearly so. I was trying to keep my audience's focus on the glory of the beauty of women! I thought I was saying something important. Today, while it might be fun to watch all the choreography, and the music may be a bit catchy with its lyrics, neither really says all that much to or about anybody but the person singing. "Look at me" is and will always be so much less interesting than "Look at her!"

On the other extreme, take a look at someone like Willie Nelson. Now there's a cat who has *lived every word of his songs*. When he sings, he is the real thing! You can see it on his face, you can hear it in his voice, you can feel it in your heart.

His song "Always on My Mind"—well, anyone who hears it knows *exactly* what he was talking about, because Mr. Nelson has lived life, done his thing, and learned how to capture it in song. To me, that's what it's all about.

Bottom line, I like talent, no matter what color it comes wrapped in, and no matter where the inspiration comes from. I take it as a victory that Black entertainment holds such appeal that people want to imitate it and eventually become a legitimate part of it. I don't see rap as an especially racial thing, and I don't think anyone else should, because the "Blackness" being presented has, in my opinion, little to do with any kind of street authenticity. That's why it's also possible for me to like New Kids on the Block, Britney Spears, the Backstreet Boys, *NSYNC, Vanilla Ice, the Beastie Boys, Eminem, and all the other so-called "White Rappers." To me all rap is the same color: *green*. But I love all the young energy, and I think it's great that we have progressed to the point where everyone can do everyone else's music *both ways* (as opposed to the fifties, when all the good R & B songs were restricted from mainstream airplay in favor of cover versions done by White artists).

Thank God White kids today are permitted, by the order of the culture of their own society, to cross over, to put themselves into a musical and social mix they weren't originally a part of, just as Black kids can now dominate the White pop charts and socially intermingle with White kids. White rappers to me represent social progress, the conquest of cultural territory for the sake of the good of everyone.

Many years ago I was playing a gig in Atlanta's Fulton Country Stadium and a bunch of White kids jumped on the top of the dugout and started doing the mashed potatoes and splits. I said to myself, *Now* we have real hope! Here were some well-off White kids dancing with the same look of fun on their faces I had when I was a kid and danced for the soldiers! That's as profound a lap around the circle as I've ever seen.

FOURTEEN

SHOW BUSINESS IS A DIFFICULT PROFESSION FOR ANY-
one in America who is Black and doesn't toe a certain
line. Look at Michael Jackson. I've known him since he
was seven or eight years old. I was his idol. In his first au-
dition he danced for Berry Gordon of Motown the way
he'd learned watching me. I admit he's got an unusual
lifestyle, but he has been convicted before any trial or hard
evidence has been brought against him. And Kobe
Bryant—are you telling me that his legal circus would
have gone on if he was a White man and the woman he
was accused of raping was Black? I don't think so.

And what about all the stealing that's gone on of *my* music, the sampling, the style-wrangling, the impersonation
of my showmanship? I guess it doesn't bother me all that

much because the one thing nobody can ever steal from me is my guts. If they could ever get that away from me, I'd no longer be a man. So I guess on the balance it's probably a better world with James Brown in it than not.

There are others around who constantly get a bum rap, some White, some Black. I like that Howard Stern fellow who's on the radio. I've done his show a number of times and he always makes me laugh. I don't understand what the government has against him. He's simply an entertainer. If he says things that you couldn't say in church— well, as far as I'm concerned, he's not in church when he's doing it. *Hey, government, leave him alone!*

Al Sharpton is another controversial figure I happen to like very, very much. Knowing the extent of the scrutiny any candidate for high office has to undergo, you have to watch everything about yourself as if it was under a microscope, from the cut of your suit to the length of your hair. You truly have to reeducate certain people as to your aims and personality, which always makes the attempt at running quite difficult.

For instance, White people see all Black men as spokesmen for the ghetto. Whenever anyone tries to get away from that, they don't believe it, even if it's someone like Colin Powell or Thurgood Marshall. Believe me, people like that are few and far between. Maybe that's why everybody laughed so hard when Secretary of State Powell said that he was thinking of appointing James Brown the secretary of soul and the foreign minister of funk as a way of putting a little street into the sidewalks of government. "Man," he had said to me with a hand on my shoulder, "you could have livened up things on the Hill." I don't think he was kidding.

As for the Reverend Al Sharpton, early on I think he did some great things when he helped instill some self-pride in a lot of Black and Puerto Rican kids. Some of the later, more controversial things, well, that's the Reverend Al—you can't pick and choose the parts of him you like and expect the rest to quietly disappear. No matter how well-dressed he becomes, he will always wear a bit of the ghetto on his sleeve. He's a human being, not a mannequin.

So would I endorse Al Sharpton if he ever seriously ran for president? This is a question I've been asked a million times and never really answered, but I'm going to now, and in this way: the reverend is a great speaker, a man filled with ideas and vision. Nevertheless, if the Democratic Party somehow ever gave him the number one pole position, they would be making a major mistake. And I think he knows that. Years ago, someone asked me what the difference was between a White boy and a Black boy, and I said that every Black boy knows that the chip doesn't fall too far from the block, while every White boy thinks he can be president. In other words, the Black boy knows the realities of his racial history, while the White boy believes just by virtue of his race that he has unlimited opportunity.

For a Black man to even dream about becoming the president, he'd better be as talented as Abe Lincoln. You understand what I'm saying? I think you do. And if this Black person does become president, he'd better stay out of Ford's Theatre!

The Reverend Sharpton's truer—and safer—role is that of a gadfly rather than a candidate. So, no, I wouldn't endorse him. However, and this is a major however, I fully endorse and support his *right* to run.

December 7, 2003, is a day I'll never forget. It was the day I was honored by the Kennedy Center for the Performing Arts in Washington, D.C., the culmination of a week-long series of events to honor lifetime achievements in culture. Honored along with me that day were Carol Burnett, Mike Nichols, Loretta Lynn, and Itzhak Perlman: an actress, a comedian turned director, and three musicians. I think that says something pretty wonderful about our country.

To me, being honored went far beyond my musical contributions, beyond the applause I got just for showing up. It was really all about the level of respect I was being shown. That night, I had the sense that I was, finally, a legitimate part of the cultural makeup of the United States of America. It was so overwhelming it brought tears to my eyes. This was all I've ever wanted in my life, to be accepted and to be acknowledged not as a Black legend, but simply as a man.

I was in the presence of greatness that night, once more allowed to stand among the country's most prominent leaders. Now I could add to the list of presidents I had personally known, a list that included Lyndon Johnson, Richard Nixon, Gerald Ford, Jimmy Carter, Ronald Reagan (someone who had such a winning persona, I really loved him), George H. W. Bush, and Bill Clinton.

What made the night so special for me was being beautifully acknowledged by these men of history for my own place in it, for who I was as much as for what I had done. At one point during the ceremonies, I couldn't help but flash on the fact that thirty-five years ago, I had come to the same district to help quell a dangerous race riot that was threatening to tear the country apart. How different this night was in every way! Here I was, privileged to be sitting with the Bushes on one side of me and the Clintons and Kennedys on the other. That made me feel especially good, because that elite group was a perfect blend of rich and poor America. Two wealthy, historically prominent families— the Kennedys and the Bushes—and the Clintons, who had made it on their own. At that moment, I could see my reflection in all of them. I, too, had attained a measure of wealth and fame, but also was this poor boy from the South who once shined shoes and tap-danced for pennies.

Mr. Clinton, an Arkansas boy, is also a personal friend of mine. Mr. Clinton did something that at the time seemed nearly impossible, which was to keep the country from going broke during peacetime. Think about that. And he was from the Democrats, the party that doesn't have nearly the financial resources and backing of the Republicans. He managed to overcome all of that, despite the nonsense about the intern and whatever else they tried to get him with. If he wasn't perfect, hey, then neither am I, and as it says in the Bible, let he who is without sin cast that first stone.

But I also liked President George W. Bush because, among other things, he has, to a degree, practiced a policy of inclusion with Black people. I like the fact that he works with Condoleezza Rice and Colin Powell.

I liked President Bush's daddy, the first President Bush, and Mr. Reagan and Mr. Carter and Mr. Ford and Mr. Nixon.

I was happy that night, happier than I had been in a very long time. In many ways, I felt as if I had reached a pinnacle. Everybody around me told me how proud they were of me, and how they shared the happiness of this great moment. I smiled and nodded my head in agreement. But only I knew how difficult it had been to get to this point.

After a lifetime of ups and downs, of bounds and rebounds, only a few months before this night I had found myself engulfed in one of the worst emotional lows in life. What kicked this latest visit to the low valley was yet another episode of financial desperation, the result of a long-time legal dispute over my music publishing. Because of all my problems with the IRS, I had no real money saved; and as I had not had a hit record in a while, not a lot of money was coming in. One day I looked around and realized that after all this time, and after all that I had accomplished, I still really didn't have anything in the way of security for the future. The bottom line was that my life had been surrounded by those characters who had come to take and not to give.

On top of that, I had recently ventured once more into the world of matrimony. Having gotten over the tragedy of Adrianne's death, and not wanting to face the last years of my life alone, I decided that the time had come to find myself a companion. I was ready to meet someone new, and fall in love again, and that's exactly when I met a young singer, Tomi Rae, who was working the rooms in Las Vegas doing an act based on the life of Janis Joplin.

Although the attraction between Miss Rae and me was strong, I was hesitant to get involved with her because of the great age difference between us. I was in my sixties, and she was in her late twenties. As a general rule, I would warn against anyone marrying a person with more than a ten-year age difference. It almost never works. It is difficult to find things to talk about, to use similar reference points, and to operate at the same speed of life. Another problem is that both sides usually don't want the same things at the same time.

Children, for instance. It's very difficult to be the father of even one child in a man's life. I happen to be the father of many, but with a younger woman, the talk inevitably turns to starting a new family, and it's hard to go down that road all over again after you've seen your children from earlier marriages grow into adulthood. When a man is older, he has a tendency to feel he has done his part. He wants to relax and spend time with just his woman. A young girl, however, has all that ahead of her. This is an issue couples have to be straight on and agree on before they walk down that aisle; otherwise there is no way their marriage will survive.

Ironically, one of the biggest issues between Adrianne and me had been children. We both wanted them but couldn't seem to have them. I had built a beautiful home for her and the family we had both hoped to have. I had wanted her to feel she was living with an ambassador, which, in many ways, I had become. For myself, I never needed much. I could just as easily live in a small place and that would be just fine with me, but I wanted her to feel that she had the best.

Now, having married Tomi Rae Brown, I once again, much to my amazement, wanted children. And happily, so did she. We started living together in the big house in South

Carolina, but soon discovered a host of new problems neither of us had anticipated, although I shouldn't have been
surprised—I had been down this road before. People
seemed disturbed by our pairing. Everyone was always
friendly to our faces, but the elephant in the room was that
I was Black and she was White, and there was no way that
was ever going to go by unnoticed—even by some of my so-
called closest friends, on both sides of the color line.

Show business has always been the one place where
race never seemed to get in the way of talent. At least not
for me. I decided to add Mrs. Rae Brown to the Revue, and
we had a lot of fun onstage. However, the gap between
our ages soon proved to be a problem for the both of us.

Remember Anna Nicole Smith's "controversial" marriage? There are similarities I see between what happened
to her and what happened with Mrs. Rae Brown and me.
Here was Anna Nicole Smith, a young and beautiful
woman, who gave herself to this older man and stayed
with him until the day he died (I'm sure with a smile on his
face). I know everybody thinks she did it for money, but
even if that's true, so what? She made this old fellow
happy in his final days, and that in and of itself is a beautiful thing. She was his angel of love, his angel of mercy,
and his angel in death, and no amount of money can buy
that kind of holiness.

I wrote many songs about love, but the best, I think,
was also the simplest. You know how it goes: *"It's a man's*

world, but it wouldn't be nothin' without a woman or a girl."
To that end, it's important to be with someone who understands your life. I believe Anna Nicole Smith understood
her husband's life, and because Tomi Rae Brown is a musician, I believe she understands mine.

Of course, the fact that she's beautiful, well, there is
also that sugar and spice I love to sing and write about!

Still, it was also hard to avoid the fact that we were from
two completely different heritages. She's Norwegian and I
am my own trail mix, and because of it there was little we
had that we could talk about without trying to cross some
high degree of generational and social hurdles. No matter
what, those barriers were always going to be there. And
because of it, I could never completely get into Tomi Rae
Brown's head, nor she into mine. But that didn't stop me
from trying to teach her about what it meant to share a life
with someone, and how to keep the fires burning inside,
now and in the future.

One of the happiest days of our marriage was when
Tomi Rae Brown gave birth to our little baby boy. She was
now the mother of our offspring, and neither of us would
ever forget that or let the other down for the sake of our
child. And both of us vowed never to forget that.

That's why, for all the generational and cultural barriers
that we had to break through as a couple, I never regretted
a single moment of being with her, even when the unusual
circumstances of our marriage thrust me back into the

tabloid's firing line. I've always believed that my private life should be my private life, and not fodder for the curious. I've always tried to suppress the flow of detailed information about my marriage, and to hide my wives and children from the constant glare and interference. What goes on in a marriage should be between husbands and wives. It isn't anybody else's business. Unfortunately, that doesn't stop the press from hounding celebrities every minute of the night and day. It's a funny thing about America. We have a tendency to eat our own.

That's why the one time Tomi Rae Brown and I got into a serious squabble, it took a two-second 911 call—*and that's all it took*—to take what was essentially a private misunderstanding and turn it into one more public James Brown debacle, in which the press tried, convicted, and sentenced me without so much as a word of my side of the story. In that sense, for all that I had accomplished in my life, for me and for my people, nothing really had changed. I was reminded all over again how easy it is in this country for a man, especially a Black man, to be taken by the system on the basis of a *single phone call* made in the heat of anger.

And hey, you want to know the truth? I *did* do some of the things that were reported, and admittedly, they weren't so great. And yes, I took a plea, but not because I was completely in the wrong, but because I wanted to stay out of jail this time, and see if we couldn't get beyond this crisis in our marriage. (How many newspapers printed that photo of us leaving court together, both smiling, arm in arm? As many as those that did of me looking like a maniac when I was arrested? I guess the happy-ending photo wasn't as juicy as the mug shot one, and probably wouldn't have sold as many newspapers.)

The bottom line remains true—when the Black man stands accused of anything, the trial by the press is over before the real one ever has a chance to begin. We are in America as we have always been—guilty until proved innocent. What happened that day between Tomi Rae Brown and me is ultimately between God and us, not the six o'clock news or the *National Enquirer*.

Now, as to those ongoing "troubles" in our marriage, I'm going to let Tomi Rae Brown tell you herself about our relationship. These are her words, told to Mr. Eliot, reproduced here just as she said them to him in our home. You judge for yourself. Ladies and gentlemen, I give you my wife, Mrs. Tomi Rae Brown:

Our story is a simple one: we met about seven years ago, in a recording studio. James amazed me with his professionalism and knowledge of how to make a record. He looked sharp, dressed to the nines. He knew every note that everybody was playing. I had to pinch myself! Next thing I know I'm having dinner with him. Then we began dating. I became pregnant, we got married, a baby arrived, and here we are.

Being married to James Brown has been magical, trying, difficult, and a real experience for me. I've learned a tremendous amount about culture, the music business (some of which I wish I hadn't learned, such as all the negative spin that is put on cultural differences, or the real, not-so-glamorous lives of writers and musicians). I always had a dream, ever since I was a little girl, to be a performer, dreams that, as I got older I realized were rarely achievable, which makes the accomplishment of my husband so much more amazing to me. His is a once-in-a-lifetime success story.

The downside to sharing all of that with him is how many people don't want you there by his side, not just onstage, but in life. It turns you into a fighter, because you have to fight for your existence in that world of TV magnifying glasses and tabloid misinformation. In a strange way, though, what at first appears to be negative turns out eventually to be positive. I thank the people for all the negative press. If they hadn't found out, say, that I hadn't been properly divorced, I never would have known it and never would have been legally married to James Brown today, which, by the way, I am.

Still, it caused problems between us. James is a very righteous man, and did not want to live with a woman who was legally married to someone else. It was the cause of a lot—but not all—of the tension between us, and which the press had an inaccurate but rollicking field day with. The lesson is, when you're married to James Brown, life, by necessity, is all about putting up the public armor even as you work to turn all the negatives into positives. I have James Brown to thank for helping me learn to do that.

Is it difficult living day to day with a legend? Very! Artists by their nature are prone to more acute mood swings than the rest of us. They are more idiosyncratic in their behavior, more eccentric. My husband is several decades older than I am, from a different time. It's like being with a husband, a best friend, and a father all melded into one. Sometimes it's hard for both of us to be in sync over which role we are playing on any given day. I'm a Generation-X person and James doesn't understand some of the things that women my age think are cool but that he sees as unladylike, such as performing, being out on my own, and really what it comes down to is having independence of thought. Women of my generation were not brought up to define their existence solely in terms of their husbands.

The best part of all, I think, is getting to watch him up close on the stage. He is the consummate performer, and that makes me want to be the best I can be. And when we're not out performing, I get to stay at home with him, listening to music together in our *room, or working on songs and dance moves for the shows. He loves to break things down, like compli- cated steps, to show me how they work. Then he puts them back together and restores the magic for me. He is the best teacher in the world!*

Finally, I wish that people would not focus so much on what the press says about my husband and me, be- cause most of it is not true. Our life together is decid- edly unsensational. We're simple people, homebodies who like to work hard and have fun together. We love each other very much. It's not about age, or money, or race, or professional status. We don't choose who we love; we love who we choose. I choose to love him, and we have vowed not to let the press destroy that.

· · ·

James Brown is a good man and a good husband, even if every once in a while it becomes a rough ride. I thank God He has given me the strength to hang on and to make this work. He is magical to be with—get that, National Enquirer? *Magical!*

Not long after I married Tomi Rae Brown, I began to have all kinds of physical problems. Added to the increas- ingly tenuous financial state that I was in, my tolerance level hit an all-time low. The one lesson I had never learned about women flunked me again: don't take your troubles out on the one you love, if you want her to keep on loving you. The fourth Mrs. Brown was young, high-strung, and unwilling to put up with my stuff. And by the beginning of 2003, we had temporarily separated.

I took that breakup particularly hard. Along with all my other ailments, an aching heart was something difficult for me to bear. At one point I felt so bad I prayed to God to take me. I had had enough and didn't want to suffer any longer. I thought nothing else could possibly happen to me in my life—I had done it all, seen it all, won it all, and lost it all. Then I got a call from my doctor—the bad news was that I had developed diabetes. The emotional plunge I took was Olympian. Imagine those divers you see going off the high board, all the way to the bottom of the pool. That was me.

Fortunately, the divers are always able to come back to the surface, and that's exactly what happened. Diabetes turned out to be one of the best things that ever happened to me. The doctors made it very clear that if I didn't live correctly from that point on, I would in fact die, simple as that. That was my cue to get off my rear end, stop feeling sorry for myself, stop taking out my frustrations on those closest to me, and help myself get back to where I needed to be. I decided to get my physical body back into prime condition through a lot of hard work, healthier living, and positive thinking.

The first thing I needed to do was lose weight. If any-body had seen a photo of me in the last few years, then they knew I had put some on. I immediately made adjustments, changed my diet, cut out the junk and the time of the day that I ate it, eliminating all those tempting midnight snacks. The pounds fell off, and within weeks, I was able to get down again to my fighting weight. I also had to adjust when I ate before or after shows. I realized I was eating too much afterward, when I didn't need all that energy. Before the show, when I normally didn't eat, was actually the best time to do so, to fuel up my system so that I had some energy to burn up on the stage.

Once I started feeling better physically, I knew that my emotional rebound was possible.

That rebound couldn't have come at a more perfect time, for while I was feeling better, there were still some very real problems I had to face. Once again, the IRS and I found ourselves at loggerheads.

I'll never understand how, in a free country, for every hundred dollars I might make, somehow or other, I get to keep about fifteen of it while eighty-five goes to the State. I don't mind, if that's the way it's done for everybody. But somehow, I feel that it is just another form of governmental control, and the more I complain about it, the bigger the bite seems to get.

I'm not just crying in my own beer. I remember Willie Nelson, a White country act, a very good man and a dear friend, who was trying to raise all that money for the farmers, and in doing so saying some pretty hard stuff about the government—well, the next thing he knew, the IRS had taken every cent. He had to fight for years to keep that one beat-up guitar. There's something wrong with that . . . something very wrong.

As far as I was concerned, I never cared about how much they took from me, as long as they didn't hound me for more than I had. But now I realized that they could never touch the things that were truly of value in my life: my beautiful home, my great children, my wonderful wife, and my loyal friends. I could still get up onstage and do some splits, wear the cape, and sing from the soul. That's when I knew the government could take every cent of mine and I'd still be the richest man in America! As soon as I had that realization, I knew that I had come back once more from the brink. And the very next week, I was told that I was to be honored by the Kennedy Center.

FIFTEEN

I AM AND ALWAYS HAVE BEEN A PERSON WHO SEEKS knowledge and the company of good people, although neither one is easy to find. That is not to say that everybody isn't good. I believe all people have a measure of goodness in them, but sometimes the ship of their life goes off course and they can't get it back together.

What is maybe even worse is that our heroes are being systematically destroyed. That happens whenever someone with influence tries to take a stand that others may not like. I can cite so many in my lifetime: Dr. King, Malcolm X, John F. Kennedy, dear brother Bobby, the countless nameless and faceless soldiers who died in Vietnam, and the ones dying today in the Middle East who were willing to put their lives on the line to defend the system of democracy.

In my own life, I've experienced a certain type of prejudice against the perception of being some kind of hero for Black men in America, as well as other parts of the world. Whether it's fear or jealousy or who knows what else, the authorities have always been a little too quick on the trigger to do what I call "containment." Think of the Indians and the White man in America. Think of the Aborigines in Australia. Think of the Black man brought here as a slave, until he was freed and then what do you do with him? Give him power and influence? I don't think so! If you can't get rid of the person himself—and you can count on the fact that I'm going to be around like the most stubborn weed in the garden—then the only other way to go is to discredit that person. My only defense is to stand by who and what I am, and to take all the bad with the good, because it comes as a package. And to try to let my music and my social influence, whatever they may be, speak for themselves.

As I get older, I am frequently asked what changes were necessary for me as a performer to stay relevant, what differences I see in the audiences and in myself. My answer may surprise you. In a word: nothing! That's right. I can't speak for audiences, except to say that they continue to show up to see me perform and I'd like to believe they don't go home disappointed. I have always given a top-of-the-line performance, like Frank Sinatra used to. He had the ability and the desire to bring his audience along with him wherever he went, especially to that part of his life that was so vitally connected to his music. That is how he allowed himself and his fans to grow together, gracefully, getting a little grayer around the temples as they continued to feed off of one another. Essentially, Sinatra always remained at heart what he was: a great singer who knew how to put on a great show, one who connected straight from his soul to everyone in the audience.

There are others of course, who could do the same thing—B. B. King comes immediately to mind, the great Aretha Franklin, and Etta James, among so many others. They are to be applauded and respected for their ability to go the distance.

Everything has a way of finding its own balance, and I believe that longevity for a performer such as myself keeps me current—things change, events change, the social milieu shifts, and therefore, the performer must change. If I don't, then I become the one thing I will never be—a memory trick, a nostalgia act, holding up the rear on some sad and pathetic oldies show.

As for keeping up and current, that's been the easiest thing of all. I've seen more changes in my lifetime than most younger performers ever will, ironically thanks to me and others like me who fought the good fight against racism so hopefully they won't have to. I bring all of that inherent drama, triumph, and history onto the stage with me every time I perform. When I break into "Please Please

Please," the very next time I sing it will be just as powerful, fresh, and invigorating as it was the first time.

This is what I hear all the time. It's not something I'm making up—people will see me before a show and come to talk to me, wondering how much of the "real," meaning, I suppose, the "young," James Brown they're going to get on any given night. I'll let you in on something. I'm seventy-two, and I don't feel anything close to fifty. I live the same way I always have: for tomorrow, while struggling through today. It keeps me going, it keeps me hungry, it keeps me strong. That's why it brings a smile to my face whenever people ask, Can you still do those splits? Or, Can your voice still hit those rough notes? Are you still into it? Do you still care about the old songs?

After the show, the big revelation from these very same people is always the same: they can't wait to tell me how much *better* I was. The reason is simple. To this day, I always bring everything I have with me onto the stage. I don't wear any makeup other than the years of living that are etched onto my face. That's the real me up there, for better or for worse.

In an odd way, despite all my years of performing, I still feel a little tightness when appearing before mixed audiences. It's like a new thing for me. That's why, I guess, for me it's as new and as fresh as it is for my fans, and if possible, it's even more exciting today than in the beginning.

In the summer of 2004, I embarked on a new world tour, one of the highlights of which was getting to meet England's royal family. In addition to playing all over Europe—Italy, where, by the way, I did my thing at the same opera houses Mario Lanza and Pavarotti did theirs; Wales; lots of outdoor festivals; and other large venues—we did a special show outside of Buckingham Palace, part of the Olympic torch ceremonies, which were taking place. Out of all the performers who were there—and there were many, many on hand—I was the only one that Princess Anne came over to speak to. I guess she remembered when Geronimo met the queen!

There I was, on the royal carpet, amid all the respect and dignity they had, and then, suddenly, here comes this lovely woman who happens to be the princess! What can I say? From Augusta to the White House to the Kennedy Center to Buckingham Palace. Not bad for a poor Black boy.

I thank God that I have attained this level of international stardom. It's a certain kind of gratification I don't think a lot of performers, especially in pop music, get to experience. It allows me to discover new places and new fans that I have never been to or played for before. As long as they want me, if I can walk, if I can talk, if I can dance, and if I can sing, I'm going out there to play for the people who want to see me. It's not an obligation but a privilege that brings me great personal joy. I still cherish the inner feeling of satisfaction I get from it, a certain special kind of ecstasy. All over the world, I have found that audiences are the same, and therefore, so am I. There is an international language of music that we all speak, and I try to say things that have meaning for everyone.

And I still love to teach by example all those poor kids out there who think the only way out of the ghetto is through lawlessness and gangs and violence. My goal is to show them there is another way. I always ask my audiences to check their anger at the door, because there's nothing to be angry about in the world of James Brown. Sometimes during a performance, I have them turn to their left and then to their right and shake the hand of the person next to them as a way to promote a new friendship.

One of the biggest differences I notice whenever I'm abroad is something that always strikes me. America, bless her heart, is still divided into two countries—a Black America and a White America. Europe, on the other hand, is moving toward consolidation—to a unified society—and I have to say, that looks to be the way of the future. They're going one world, while we're still stuck in the divided racist mire of the past.

In addition to unity, I'm also preaching a theme of self-motivation in my shows; I want kids to see a man in his seventies doing what I do and have them leave afterward with the feeling that hey, if he can do it, I can do it better!

Whenever they ask me how to break into my world, I tell them first to finish with theirs—to stay in school and get an education and then, if they want to try the world of show business, make sure they have the talent, the ability, and the perseverance. It's a yellow brick road to be sure, but it's filled with potholes and detours and dead ends. So I tell them to be prepared!

Unlike a lot of big stars today, I believe in signing autographs because, for kids especially, that signature becomes a kind of contract, a memento of a moment shared, a talisman of sorts to remind them of what they can achieve if they apply themselves. No matter how tired I am after a show, I always try to make time for the youngsters, to reach out to them personally and let them know that James Brown is as real off the stage as he is on. It's especially gratifying to me when I'm going through an airport, and a little kid sees me and gets excited. That tells me something about my impact on the world that very few descriptions can match. I thank God for it.

No matter where I travel to in the world—and I've been everywhere by now—my favorite place remains my adopted hometown, Augusta, Georgia. There's a special magic that takes place whenever I perform there, because I'm one of their own, and like the Crusaders of old, I always return triumphant from the big battles.

A lot of people don't realize what a center of R & B

Augusta really was. In the early years, the big Northern cities had a tendency to snub the small towns, where a lot of the music actually came from. I don't really know why. Maybe they wanted all the glory for themselves; maybe they didn't want to build up the South too much in their mind. But I'll tell you this: once I moved to New York City and had those Liberty license plates on my cars, everybody laughed at me whenever I drove back. They knew I wasn't a city boy—just a homey who had made it big and moved up north for a while to hang out with the show business crowd.

The result was that once I had relocated to Queens, I really had no home. Suddenly I wasn't from anywhere! I had left the South, but I was never what anybody would ever mistake for a New Yorker. I was born in the South, I'm a Southern boy, and I'll die in the South.

Living in or near Augusta is also good for the town, because in show business, stars follow stars. If I put on a show here, all of a sudden a lot of performers who would never think of coming to Augusta will suddenly book a night or two. It's a very good thing for the city, and a very nice tip of the cap to me.

Let me share a secret with you. I really don't get paid a lot of money for performing in down-home affairs. After all the band members and offstage crew and transportation is provided for, there isn't that much left. I have a concept of my show, what it should look and sound like, and I never cut corners. Whatever money I do make, I try to keep my contributions up for the causes I believe in, most of all for underprivileged kids. I don't like to make a big deal out of it, but it's something I believe in and something I am proud of.

It's another way of saying that my life has never been better!

I do have some advice for all the single guys out there, especially the ones who want to be artists, or performers, or in some other aspect of the entertainment industry. If you're single, you'll have a better chance of being around for a long time. If you marry, your career will likely be cut short. The most successful people in the business don't marry until later in their careers, when they're ready to make that major change in their lives. And the ones who have the crushes on you in the audience, the ones who buy the records, tend to lose a certain type of interest when they know your life offstage is different from the one you're projecting to them. I'm not saying never get married. I'm just saying keep your priorities straight.

Another thing I know about and want to share with you is the power of prayer. I pray a lot these days, even more so than when I was a younger man. Religion means more to me now. I've seen it all and done it all. I've made friends with presidents, emperors, and kings, and I don't envy any of them. They are, in a certain way, cursed by the power they have. They come to believe they are gods, of a sort, although of course they aren't really at all. Me, I *come from*

God, I am always trying to serve Him, because that is where the true power lies. I don't envy anybody for who they are or what they have, you see, because I have the blessing of God and there isn't anything more sacred or priceless or powerful than that. Maybe that's the real reason they call me the Godfather of Soul.

I not only continue to identify with many of the stories of the Bible, but I believe my life story and therefore my destiny come directly out of the Good Book. It's why I've never been afraid or worried about what anybody else thinks of me or what I've done or what I do. There's nothing left to prove to anyone. I have lived my life the way I wanted to, and that remains my biggest hit, my greatest victory.

The one person I feel the closest to in the Bible, a true kindred spirit (and I mean this in the most humble of ways), is Moses, because I still feel the need to help my people find a better place in this world, and I do it by looking up and asking for advice from the Almighty. Whatever talent and joy He has given to me, I feel it was for a purpose, and that purpose has never changed: to make others happy, to make them feel good, to make them feel proud of who they are, and to help in the cause of freedom for all men and women, regardless of their race, color, or creed. It's really that simple. And that deep.

The pen is mightier than the sword. It's an old cliché, I know, but it's true. My words have kept me alive, brought me everything in life, and my melodies and rhythms have dressed them up in their Sunday best. There's no doubt that when I started, the field of battle for the civil rights movement in America was just about everywhere—in the schools, at the workplace, in the movies, and in music. I'm proud to say that I was a soldier in that war, and while victory may not yet be complete, I know that I came out of many a battle with my head held high, proud to have survived. You win a war in many different ways. Remember, when the civil rights movement began, it was about a small percentage of the population that had no money, no representation, no power, no influence. And look what happened.

Today, a lot of young Black people don't have a clue as to what went on just before they arrived on the scene, or the price that was paid to win the degree of freedom they now have in America. I see Prince, and I see Michael Jackson, and I love them both, but I also know that if I didn't lay down the foundation, they might not be the performing royalty that they are today, especially among White audiences.

Before me, the Black man in mainstream entertainment was still the standard house Negro. *Yassir, no sir, may I sir, oh thank you, massah.* How White folks loved those Negroes! Take a look at any Hollywood film made before the end of World War II and you can't help but see how this country treated its Black people. Butlers. Maids. Mammys. Cooks. Houseboys. Uncle Toms. Slaves. Mandingos. Criminals. Mental retards. In all the years mainstream

White Hollywood had been making movies, not a single Black man before Sidney Poitier had ever been allowed to romance a woman, Black or White. Or play the hero. Or be smarter than anyone else. Or dress in a suit that didn't have tails on it to make him look like a penguin, or an apron and a hair wrap for the women. Onscreen, Blacks were considered less of a human being. I'm not making this up—it's all there—and because of the nature of film, it will always be there—a reminder of how America regarded its African-American populace. You can't hide it and you can't pretend it didn't exist, because it's as close as your nearest DVD rental store or cable TV movie channel.

And it's not just true for Blacks. Hollywood never knew what to make of the Chinese—smart? Dumb? The Spanish were always the Latin lovers with no money and no prospects; Mexicans were always bandits; Indians were yelping, ignorant alcoholic savages; and Asians were bizarre servants walking around in diapers and turbans. And most of them were played by White men and women. Hollywood wouldn't hire real Indians or authentic Spaniards because, they said, they didn't look enough like who they were supposed to be! They'd make up White men with horses' tails and call it "Indian hair." And it wasn't much better on TV. Where was the Black Jack La Lanne? Or the Black Charles Atlas? Or the Black Ed Sullivan? Or the Black David Letterman? *Oh brother!*

In sports, it's harder to see because for the longest time

there simply were no professional Black athletes. Today, of course, sports have been elevated by the presence of the Black athlete. Every game we play in, we play better. Sports have given us the belief that if we compete fairly, train hard and play to our capacity, we can win. And all of America, Black and White, will cheer us for it.

Someday, gays will look back on Hollywood at all the swishing that they had to endure, and wonder why anybody would let that kind of stereotyping go on for so long!

Of course, once we—meaning Black performers—crossed the line, we could see our remnant shadows in the best of them! Elvis Presley, Mick Jagger, and Bruce Springsteen for openers, and then all the thousands who followed in their wake who emerged from the great encompassing Black Shadow of American culture. That is why I'm proud to still be standing, proud to be able to say it loud, proud to say that I am Black and I am proud. And that is why I thank God every day that young kids, White and Black, still discover me and believe in me. It humbles me that they get joy from my music the way I once did from Louis Jordan's.

And while I appreciate the Kennedy Center Awards, and all the accolades from the industry bigs and the legendary performers, what matters to me most is that kids are still turned on by me. In the end, I'm really the messenger, not the message. I'm the messenger of something that has become very important in our country as a symbol of freedom. We are fortunate to be living in a time when, while listening to my music and the music of others, White girls no longer have to be afraid to look at Black boys, and Black boys don't have to fear the consequences of looking at White girls. And if they happen to want to dance together, they don't have to worry that someone is going to come in the night, take them away, and lynch them from the highest tree. Freedom is the message contained in the music of James Brown, the ultimate freedom-fighting messenger.

So yes, I remain the so-called Hardest-Working Man in Show Business. People know who James Brown is, because James Brown knows who the people are. That is why they keep coming, and why I'm still going. That sense of optimism everyone gets from me when they see the James Brown Revue is from the happiness and energy that emerges from within it.

The most difficult thing to do in show business, especially rock and roll and all its component parts—soul, funk, R & B, and hip-hop—is to know when the right time has come to hang up your blue suede shoes. The key to it is knowing whether people are going to miss you when you hang those shoes up. If they don't, you've been around too long. If they do, you did it right. You knew there were things you could no longer do, and didn't try to do them. So much of the harder edge of my kind of music is directly connected to the sexuality of both the performer and the listener, and once a certain point has passed, it no longer makes much sense to continue to try to be some-body you aren't.

That's why pop singers can last a lot longer. Their appeal is softer, and they can age more gracefully. Look at Frank Sinatra, Pat Boone, great pop singers like that. Some of the grizzled blues men can do it, too, especially when they look as if they were never young, but for the real soul brothers and sisters, the funk gang, and all the rest of them, a hard look and sex appeal are intertwined, and the music doesn't make a lot of sense without it. The day I hear a titter from the audience when I do "Sex Machine" is the day I know I've been doing it too long.

As I grow older, I've started thinking about these things more and more. There was more than one time I decided that maybe all the hassle just wasn't worth it.

I took a trip to Rome during one of my down periods a few years ago, and had the good fortune to be greeted by the pope. The pontiff shook my hand three times; then we talked and I told him I had been thinking about leaving the music business, and to my surprise, he advised against it. I asked him why. He said, "Because, sir, you can get things done." Those words stayed with me, and gave me the conviction to go back and try to better my life, and the lives of those I influence. The pope convinced me that I still could.

But let's face facts. The twentieth century is history. I have my place in it. Others who came before me had to toe a certain line that I trampled over, and did so proudly.

I never looked for the White audiences—they looked for me. And I will be forever grateful for that. This is now the twenty-first century. A new day. A new dawn. A new era of entertainment that leads to cultural change and social growth. Let's hope it doesn't turn into another negative hootenanny, but stays positive and becomes another kind of leap forward for mankind. Let's put all these wars behind us and live like brothers. We need to get down now. Each of us needs to give a little to the cause of peace and freedom for all the men and women of this Earth. We need to be generous and hospitable. We need to stop bleeding our good people of everything they have earned with their hard work and the sweat of their souls for the good of the greedy few and instead feed the hungry and tend to the sick. We must use what we have to help others. That's right. We must all try to live together, man and wife, brothers and sisters. We've got to try to make this world right. We've got to make life a celebration rather than a war.

SIXTEEN

A T THE AGE OF SEVENTY-TWO, I KNOW ENOUGH TO realize I can't change the world. And you know what? That's fine with me. I have nothing left to prove. I go out and do shows now just for the sheer joy of performing! At threescore and ten and counting, I have lived all the years that God allotted me. I've lived every moment as hard and as strong as I could, and I've survived! From here on, it's all gravy! I am the most grateful man in the world, still curious, still full of the wonder of it all.

I have been blessed to see incredible things, and some that were not so great. The world is still at war and there are strong, sometimes hostile political feelings in the air. However, there is one thing that remains as positive as ever, something that I know unifies people everywhere and can possibly even save this planet. That thing is music.

The main problem, as I see it, is that we're in the same old situation that stems from a generational problem. Young people still don't listen to their elders. They never did! Not on a family level, and not on the planet where lives the family of man. I believe that only music can bring that family together. Music remains the mother of the children of the world.

I intend to continue on my life's journey, and hope that audiences of all colors and nationalities will continue to give me the chance to entertain them. With Mr. Bobbit by my side, I will go around the world at least one more time with the Revue. As much as I need to continue to perform, it is my hope that the world of popular entertainment, in one form or another, still needs me.

Anybody who knows me will tell you that I'm as ready as ever to still get on that big train and ride! What I'd like to do next is to go against the current grain of the music industry, a time when downloading and file sharing has gotten the record companies a little crazy. Maybe I'm wrong but I feel if the music they were putting out was good enough, people would be going down to the stores and buying it. I don't know if it could be any simpler than that. And it is because of that truth that my plan is to start a new record company, on the order of King Records, in a city not primarily known for its music, away from the big honchos—say Cincinnati. I'd record my own new music and find the young talent around and capture what is *really* going down today, in the ghettos, in those pockets that the mass market big boys haven't as yet figured out how to turn into the latest T-shirt or brand of soft drink.

If the industry is really crying out for a savior, brothers and sisters, here I am! With Mr. Bobbit by my side to handle the finances, and me in the studio, we'd get it right and inject some real energy and meaning into the world of music in these new times. We'd be the first mom-and-pop record company of the twenty-first century! It can be done, and for not a lot of money. Talent is the key, and that's always out there, waiting to be discovered. The circle of music will not be broken, even if, as they say in the *Godfather* movie, it would be difficult, but not impossible!

I'd also like to get the chance to reintroduce the concept of radio as I knew it when I was a kid so that every youngster, rather than being exposed to the commercial products rammed down his throat on the airwaves twenty-four hours a day, can be connected, positively, to the voices and the music of his generation.

I'm also very much into the concept of holograms, which I believe to be the next step in videos, so that you can actually see a James Brown performance in 3-D in your home, from all different angles, without wearing special glasses or anything. It's very exciting to me. As always, I believe in the future.

But most of all I want to help young people to understand the importance of *believing in themselves*. Then, try to earn a living with your art. Always honor your mother and father, and choose a way to God, any path you want as long as you have one. Even when you make it, if you're that lucky, I would say to invest your earnings in something that will always provide a backup. If I were starting out today I'd go into the heating and air-conditioning field. These are two things everyone needs and always will need. It could provide plenty of income between those hit songs, or those big bookings. I'd say don't spend your money on just the girls (or the boys) and the good times; create something for yourself that will provide income for you for when the hits stop coming.

Finally, I want to say one thing. I still have my faith, I still have my integrity, I still got my funk, and I still got my soul. I love my children and I love my wife very much, and I know that she is going to be all right because she's young and has a lot ahead of her. As for me, like Sinatra was, I'm in the prime of my life in my early seventies, and it's better now than it's ever been. Nothing about living to me is trivial. Money or fame, nothing can touch me in a bad way. As long as I have three things—my health, my integrity, and my family—nothing else really matters. I will never be brought down, because I *can't* be brought down. I have a pride that cannot be broken, that cannot be trampled.

They can take me anywhere they want to, put me anywhere they think they have to, but they'll never get me to
the one place that will mean they have won—to my knees.
No, sir. Never. Because God made me in such a way that I
will never surrender.

Each and every one of you out there, listen to James
Brown. Take a spoonful of mineral oil every day and you'll
live for two hundred years. And if you do, I hope that I
live two hundred years minus one day, so I never know
that beautiful people like you have passed away. I mean
that from the bottom of my heart and the depths of my
soul.

I want to thank my longtime manager and dear friend,
Mr. Charles Bobbit. We've been together more than thirty
years, and I must say he has proved time and time again to
be nothing less than an angel. I can't put it any simpler or
better than that. When he's not with me I feel something
is missing, and when he's home and I'm not around, his
family keeps asking him what's wrong. We are that close. I
trust him with my life, and equally important, I trust him
with my wallet! Seriously, Mr. Bobbit has been with me
from my earliest days at the Apollo, all the way through
working on this book. A lot of record companies won't hire
Black executives because they think they can't handle the
job, or that they're dishonest, or whatever. They don't
know the advantages of having someone like Mr. Bobbit,

who knows the business end of music as well, if not better, than I do. There are only two qualifications—business smarts and honesty. And one more thing: the ability to let the talent do what they know how to do. Just remember, you can have the fanciest fleet of cars in the world, but if you do, you better have the best fleet of mechanics to keep them running.

For many years, at night, after a show, Mr. Bobbit and I would sit around and talk about things, and I've often wondered if I would someday be able to tell my story the way it should be told, with all the important stuff put in and all the unimportant stuff left out. When I met the right person to help me, Mr. Marc Eliot, I knew I had found the right one. He has become a truly great friend. He's a real man's man, this Eliot—a left-handed New York White cat who's got it all together and tells it like it is. Brave dude. And ladies, he's good-lookin' with great hair and real teeth, so you better look out!

I also want to thank my beautiful wife, Mrs. Tomi Rae Brown, for all the love there is between us, and for contributing her thoughts to this book.

I also want to thank Super Frank, Intrigue Music, all the good folks up at the William Morris office, and all the kind people at New American Library, especially my editor, Mr. Dan Slater, and all those good people there who had a hand in putting my book together.

I want to acknowledge the following people who have

always been there for me these many years, some longer than others: Bobby and Vicky Byrd, Ann Norman, Johnny Terry, Bob Patton, Willie Mae Keels, Miss Vonnie Hilton Sweeney (God rest her soul), as well as Deanna Brown Thomas and Deidre Jenkins. Many of these people also helped contribute photos to this book.

I know we'll all catch up with one another again somewhere farther down the line. I'll be looking for you, so look for me as well, because I plan on being around for a long, long time. If I make it to eighty, or even ninety-five, I'll still be up there doing my thing, putting out my music and my message, performing my show, hoping that enough people want to come to see it.

Remember, you can't beat the horse down the stretch if he's kept in the stall! You got to put him out on the track often enough to keep him in shape! Frank Sinatra did precisely that from the thirties until the nineties. He just kept on doing his thing, perfect and fresh, right up to the end. I keep him in mind every time I hit the stage. I want to be as great as he was, as long as he was. He was a true professional. He knew about taking care of *business*, and, I hope, so do I. Whenever someone says that about me, I always take it as the highest compliment there is.

So, as I live out the rest of my life, I wait like Moses for God to tell me what to do next to help lead all my people into a better world. And as I do so, I hope you can all feel like I do every day, 'cause, brothers and sisters, everybody's got soul, Black and White. That's one of the main reasons that, after all that's gone down, I can hold up my head and say I've done it all, I'm still in the saddle, I'm still smiling, and I still feel good.

So get up with me and let's all hit it on the "One"!

JB